NEVER TO GROW UP

NEVER TO GROW UP

Preventing Violence in Our Schools

By

ROBERT D. SOLLARS

iUniverse, Inc.
New York   Bloomington

Never To Grow Up
Preventing Violence in our schools

iUniverse books may be ordered through booksellers or by contacting:

iUniverse
1663 Liberty Drive
Bloomington, IN 47403
www.iuniverse.com
1-800-Authors (1-800-288-4677)

ISBN: 978-1-4401-7269-4 (sc)
ISBN: 978-1-4401-7270-0 (ebk)

Printed in the United States of America

iUniverse rev. date: 10/20/2009

Dedication

I would like to dedicate this book to several people. I feel that it was the mutual love for one another that made this project worthwhile.

First is my daughter Tasha (Natasha B'lanna). She is the apple of my eye. While only a child, she has wisdom beyond her years, and a silliness that is matched only by mine. I want her to grow up and never have to face what has happened at so many schools across the country, Columbine being only the most famous.

Second is my wife and true soul mate, Eileen (a right proper Irish name for my Irish lass). Without her tough love approach after my blindness, I wouldn't have had the courage to accomplish the things I have (ask her about walking me into a tree!). She has been the other half of my soul, my cheerleader, my counselor, my sounding board, and (unfortunately) my whipping girl when I got frustrated. I still owe her forty-three years of marriage, and I intend to live up to that, the Lord willin' and the crick don' rise!

I also need to thank two of the most complicated, intelligent beings I know—Admiral K'reme and Ensign

Boo Boo. The admiral is a domestic shorthair who has acted like a guardian cat since I went blind—such a long story—and the newest member to the family, Boo Boo is a Siamese who came to live with us just a few short months ago. Both are in a *cat*egory by themselves when it comes to providing devotion, love, and a calming effect on the savage beast (me).

Last, this is for all the children in the United States who go to school every day in fear. They are bullied and teased, surrounded by violence and drugs. I wish that I could hold and hug them and protect them all. But of course that is impossible, so I'm hoping that the people reading this book will act in my place and keep this special group safe from another Columbine or Virginia Tech.

Contents

Foreword

Just what in the heck is a foreword about, but he asked and so here I am. This book is for parents, grandparents, and anyone who works with children. We need to protect our children, and here you find out how. Robert, besides being my husband, is a security professional with decades of experience. His main focus of study has been workplace violence, especially the warning signs and attitudes that can foster it. Yet in recent years, he has noticed a similarity between what people were saying about the perpetrators of workplace violence and what they said about those of school violence. Could it be that similar situations and experiences could connect these two types of incidents? Well, his research has shown that. So in his desire to protect our children, he now presents this book.

I have been his partner in writing this book, so any errors in research are mine. Several years ago, Robert went blind. Diabetes took his sight but not his foresight, his vision of helping people understand school violence. Everyone understands the impact of violence on our children and schools, and everyone wants *the* answer for preventing school violence. Well, if *the* answer is what you are looking for, then this book isn't for you because, truthfully, there is not one answer. Each incident of school violence is different and triggered by different catalysts. Each child is different, and so each incident is different. What you need to learn is the basic whys and hows as you gain the skills you need to be able to spot children on the edge. No one has the magic answer, and if they tell you they do, run away as quickly as you can.

Introduction

DeKalb, Missouri, March 21, 1987: It was a bright, sunny day in the Buchanan County R-IV School District. Winter was over, Easter was on the way, as was spring break, and it was just a typical, cool, early spring day.

Kids were flowing into the middle school in this town with a population of 298. The town was small, but students came in from the surrounding area by the hundreds. There was a lot of laughing and talking, as you might expect of young teens.

That is until Nathan Faris entered his classroom. The chubby thirteen-year-old was on a mission. He had been bullied and teased for most of his life. But recently, one boy had been tormenting him worse than ever, and Nathan decided that today it would end.

As the tormenter entered the classroom, Nathan pulled out his father's .357 and aimed it at him. Another classmate jumped in front of the bully and took a bullet for him. Sadly, Nathan then did what he thought was the only option left to him: he turned the gun on himself and put a slug into his head.

This is the story that began it all for me. I lived in another rural school district just north of there. My son would be entering school soon, and this was too close to home. It also showed me that murder could be committed anywhere by anyone. Nathan Faris was certainly not the first to do what he did, nor was he the last, but he brought home the problem to us in sleepy and quiet northwest Missouri.

It also brought up many memories for me as well, from just a scant few years before. You see, I was the short, fat kid for more than a few years, and I was incessantly bullied and teased by others, both older and younger. And the worst of it was being teased by teachers. Yes, teachers.

It was okay for me being short and fat (five-foot-nothing and well over 200 pounds). Everything was fine until I started seventh grade. I had to go to a middle school a long way from my elementary school, so I had no friends.

Being fat was bad enough, but then my ineptitude at sports, mechanical things, and, worse, girls made me the center of bullying and teasing at Bode Middle School.

Most of my classes were fine until it came to phys Ed and shop. I was horrible at both. The teachers encouraged bullying and teasing by ridiculing me in front of the other students. This lasted through tenth grade, when I moved out of state and lost nearly sixty pounds.

So besides having been in the security field for nearly three decades, studying and researching school violence and watching in horror every time it happened, I LIVED IT! I know what it's like to be bullied and teased.

I was fortunate enough to be as naive and clueless as I was fat. I wanted to beat the hell out of some of those people but never had a death list or considered taking a weapon to school. In 1987, I was twenty-six and relived all those memories every time I read another article about Nathan.

April 20, 1999, is a date that will burn in the minds of parents, school administrators, and police forever at a school in Colorado. For those who may have forgotten and buried the memory of it in the sand, that is the date of the Columbine High School massacre.

For several terrifying hours, the teenagers, teachers, parents, and police agonized over what had happened. How many were dead? How many were injured? Who was killing our kids? How many were shooting up the school? And finally, after a few days, what will this cost us? And I do not mean financially. How many young lives were insanely ripped from their families? The cost would to never know what they could have accomplished with their lives. Did we let a future president die? Or maybe it was the person destined to cure cancer?

The point is that we are letting our kids kill and be killed while they are in the place that they should be safest except for home. And yes, I said we—all of us, everyone who has an interest in watching kids grow up and achieve. We as parents and educators bury our heads and expect

Beaver Cleaver to be at the same school as our children. Unfortunately, Beaver doesn't go to school anymore.

What used to be a small problem has now, in my estimation, become an epidemic. We'll look at the statistics in a bit. I think that you want to know who is telling you all of this information and why my ideas have been called radical and are in noncompliance with the State of Arizona.

I am not a psychiatrist, psychologist, medical doctor, or even a behavior scientist. I am a security expert. And to be completely honest, I don't even work for a school, district, or other type of educational institution. But with three kids of my own, two stepchildren, and more than twenty-six years' experience working in security, I think that I am qualified.

As you will soon see, my theories and practical applications are radically different from those of the "talking heads" in the media and even the PhDs. They have worked long and hard to get where they are; I just happen to disagree with their ideas.

One idea that we all have to get accustomed to is that, unfortunately, we cannot guarantee the safety of our kids while they are at school. No matter how hard we try, something will happen. We could turn our schools into gulags, and it would still happen.

Chapter 1

What Is School Violence?

There are a great many myths concerning violence in our schools. And that's exactly what they are—myths. We will address all of these myths in detail in the following chapters.

But what are these myths that I'm talking about? They are the founding premise of the hand-wringing we as a society do every time we have a violent incident. Keep in mind that others have created lists of this type as well. This list is not all inclusive and counts several different myths together that others have set out separately.

Myth #1—**He didn't fit the profile.**

Let me be succinct in busting this myth: *there is no profile!* While other types of violence, such as workplace violence, can be profiled, there is none for violence in our schools.

Not all school shooters are loners, losers, druggies, or other crazies. The truth is that violence in our schools is committed by virtually every category of student, from white to Asian, A student to F student, those who dress Goth to those who dress preppy.

The only consistency in school violence incidents is that the overwhelming numbers of incidents, 90 percent, are started by males. While females have committed such crimes, they seem be able to control their hormones and anger better than testosterone-laden boys.

Myth #2—**He just snapped.**

No one ever "just snaps," even if it appears so at first. There are always warning signs to tell us what is likely to happen or, at the very least, to tell us that a teenager needs help of some kind.

It is whether we ignore these warning signs or act upon them that is key. We have all seen how a type of behavior is dismissed because "That's just them" or "They are going through some stuff." *We* have to pay attention to our teenagers, family, and co-workers to see the problem. Ignoring the problem will not make it go away.

Myth #3—**No threats were ever made.**

Threats can be made in any number of ways. It doesn't have to be a finger-pointing, chest-thumping, screaming, drag-them-away type of incident to constitute a threat.

As you'll see later, there are four types of threats. They range from the silent and subtle to out-and-out threats. But just because a threat is not specifically mentioned doesn't mean that one isn't implied.

Myth #4—**If only we had …**

We can never protect our schools to an absolute degree of security. Just because we have metal detectors doesn't mean that we will catch all knives or firearms coming into the school.

Weapons can be found inside the school as well. Cafeteria utensils, pencils, scissors, and letter openers can be used.

Not even flooding the campus with resource officers is a guarantee. Remember, the massacres at Columbine and Jonesboro, Arkansas, each took less than ten minutes. A SWAT team couldn't have done any good.

Myth #5—**We did everything we could to help.**

In most cases when we hear these words from either the school or the parents, it's an out-and-out lie. No one does everything they can to stop an incident or help a troubled teen.

Another aspect we'll discuss is communication. There is never enough of it between all parties involved. Schools will tell you there is not enough money or time, and most parents are so busy with keeping up with the Joneses or paying bills that they don't have time either.

When it comes to our kids—whether it is a school, district, parents, or just interested people—there *has* to be time. If something is important enough, you make the time *and* the money for it.

Also falling into this category of myth is the most obfuscated statement I've ever heard: "My little angel would never do something like that." I am so sick and tired of hearing that from irresponsible parents! At any given moment on any given day, we are all capable of murder.

Myth #6—**Violence is not rampant.**

This is yet another load that you've been fed. Violence is actually on the upswing in our schools, whether anyone wants to admit it or not. The schools won't give you a straight answer because it makes them look bad.

While it is true that the murder rate is actually down in schools, we still lose between twenty and thirty teenagers to homicide every year. On top of that, the assault rate is rising like the *Enterprise* chasing after Romulans!

So What Is School Violence?

You may think that this is an easy question to answer. So take a shot. School violence is something that happens at a school when a child is seriously injured. Right? Well, you would be partially right. School violence does happen at school, and someone usually gets hurt. But let's expand that a bit. If children are bullied and teased on a daily basis, could they not then turn the tables on their tormentors? So bullying and teasing can be termed violence because of where they can lead. If a child is harassed outside of school by children who attend the same school, could that not erupt into a confrontation at school? So then school violence can be defined as an incident that occurs at or because of school.

Even a verbal altercation can lead to much more than you might think. An argument over a girl sparked a fatal stabbing at an off-campus bus stop in Florida in 2006. I'm pretty sure that wasn't the first murder over a high school romance. Anything can lead a coward to commit murder. I might add that many may think of this as an inner-city or minority problem, but more white students are murdered by other white kids than any other group.

And as for gang violence, that is a problem I am more than willing to leave to the police, Immigrations and Custom Enforcement (ICE), and riot police. Gangs and the violence and mayhem they cause are a problem wholly unto itself and, aside from the specific items discussed in this book, will not be addressed. But rest assured that gang affiliation causes its own set of violence inside and outside the schools.

One thing that we all have to understand and get accustomed to is that we cannot guarantee the safety of our children while they are at school. No matter how hard we try, something will happen. We could provide ten-foot-high walls with guard towers, concertina wire all around the top and around the gates, physical searches, turnstiles and cameras everywhere, security officers armed with M-16s, and double-trap vehicle gates, but it wouldn't stop all the violence. Besides, how we would pay for all this, and who would want their children going to a place like that for their education?

So how do we define what school violence is or is not? Where does the property lines of the school end, transferring the teenager problem to the city instead of the school district? Is it still school violence if it happens at the corner store on a Saturday afternoon? Or after the homecoming game at the local burger joint? Or is it within your own home? Is this a problem that extends beyond those in charge of the local high school?

The answer to all the prior questions is deceptively simple: yes. Shall I repeat it? *Yes.* Now you are under the impression that I am totally off my rocker, but trust me, you'll understand once I've explained. The succinct explanation is this: **Any incident of violence that at its root begins at school is to be considered school violence, even if the actual incident doesn't take place on school property.**

In case I've really confused you, let me explain. I'm not just talking about the children who bring weapons to school and start firing away at everybody. I'm talking about the quiet kid who, one day at the supermarket, runs over the guy who makes his life hell in gym class, the girl who poisons another at the restaurant because of a stolen boyfriend, the newly licensed SUV driver who runs an upperclassman off the road because he has been bullied one too many times in the hallway, and the boy who kills the beloved pet of his worst enemy or ex-girlfriend. These incidents don't take place on school property but happen because of school interactions.

These incidents are never reported in the media as school violence because they occur off school property. So the definition used by school administrators, psychologists, police, security officers, and the media is outdated and in need of a revision. It is not a revision needed to cause change; the changes in our society necessitate the revision.

Chapter 2

Parental Responsibility and School Accountability

Everyone seems to want to blame someone else for the problem of school violence. Psychologists blame society, conservatives blame the breakdown of family values, and liberals blame everyone and want the government to take over the whole issue.

So who is to blame? We all are—parents, the schools, the teacher unions, society at large, and of course the entertainment industry. I will explain myself shortly.

Most of us with teenaged children remember the seventies and eighties quite well. The seventies were the ME decade. We were just coming out of the hippie years and moving into the disco era. We were raised by parents who were still high on flower power. It was all about me and what I want; it doesn't matter if it's good for anyone else because it makes me feel good.

Then came the eighties, and it was all about power and greed as well as me. Take care of numero uno and no one else. By God, I'm gonna have money, power, and everything else. And we were willing to do most anything to get it.

That attitude has bled into how we've raised our children in the eighties, nineties, and now. Whether we realize it or not, our children learn very well from us.

We have raised our children with the expectation of re-wards and an ever-increasing sense of entitlement. "If you get good grades, we'll buy you a TV for your room, with cable." "Our kids only have to come out for food because of course they have their own bathroom." And then the kids who don't have rich parents are sitting there drooling and thinking to themselves, "Hell, I gotta do something to get me an iPod," and their parents feel guilty because they can't provide everything their children want.

An illustration of this point comes from a friend. Her sister was upper-middle class, and she and her husband showered their son with an ever-growing array of gadgets and gifts for doing well in school. The son was consistently among the top in his class. When the momentous occasion of his sixteenth birthday neared, he calmly and in all seriousness asked if his new Mustang would be his birthday or his Christmas present. His mother informed him that he was not getting a $25,000 car for either, which led to a verbal fight that continued when his dad got home. The son received very expensive birthday and Christmas gifts—well over $2,000 spent—but guess what? The parents felt guilty for not buying him a car.

In addition to raising our kids with a sense of entitlement, we parents, along with others, push the importance of self-esteem and self-worth too far. In the real world, we face disappointment every day. We also have to face people who will damage our self-esteem and self-worth. We are not all the same. It is a natural course of events that some of us turn out smarter than others.

It's also natural that some people are better at sports than others, just as not everyone's art project will get an A. If we keep telling our children that no one is better than anyone else, then how do we, the human race, get better? Our children are going to be sorely disappointed when they grow up.

Don't get me wrong. I believe that all children need to know that they are loved and that we have to help build their self-confidence. But telling them that a baseball or soccer game is played for the exercise only because we don't keep score is not preparing them for the very real disappointments in life. And of course we have to eliminate baseball, football, dodge ball, and tag from the playground. Why? Because children might get their feelings hurt by being tagged and because, as parents in this lawsuit-happy society, we think that when little Susie gets knocked down, it's time to sue the school and live high off the rest of the parents in the district.

If we spent a little more time worrying about why our children can't learn and less about being sued, suing, or the assorted bumps, bruises, and cuts that come with life, we would be better off. Has it occurred to anyone that letting our children run around and be a tad aggressive is a good thing? Has any thought been given to the fact that it gets rid of stress and frustration?

We all like to blame the entertainment industry, with its rap music, video games, movies, and so on. But who is really to blame for what is in those video games, CDs, and DVDs? We as parents are. Unfortunately, I'm not wrong. Let me explain a bit.

First, who buys the CDs, DVDs, and video games? Most of the time, we as parents do. You don't buy them? Then, second, who allows it into the house without checking the content? And third, who allows their children to go to their friends' houses where that type of material is accepted?

As parents, we have control over what our children see, hear, and play. That may come as a shock to some parents, but it is true. We have the right to check for warning labels, bad lyrics, and content and to block certain channels on the TV. We even have the right and responsibility to ground our children from going places where that stuff is smiled upon.

This last one is a shocker to everyone: parents even have the right to go into their teenager's room and snoop! Yes, I know that it is revolutionary concept, but it's true. And recent studies have shown that the teens don't mind if it means countering drug use.

Remember what happened after Columbine? The parents of Dylan Klebold and Eric Harris stated that they had no idea what was in their sons' rooms. If they had been better parents and snooped a bit, it could have prevented the tragedy. Children should never be allowed to have an Internet-accessible computer in their rooms. Of course, there were many other signs that the parents missed as well, not just the e-mails the boys sent.

Society at large is also at fault for our kids killing kids. Our society is accepting of a great many things. Why? Because we are becoming a nation of wimps. We are afraid of hurting someone's feelings. Or we think, "It's not my problem. If I ignore it, it will go away." Or we're afraid of being sued and even being involved in a physical confrontation.

We, as a society, need to step up to the plate and let other parents, teachers, and kids know what appropriate behavior is and what is not. That is one way to stop this epidemic of school violence.

Lastly, parents need to COMMMUNICATE with our children. Notice that I put that in big letters because this is the most important point of all. It doesn't matter how you do it—a weekly sit-down at the dinner table, during a walk in the park, while playing catch in the backyard, when you're somewhere their friends can't see. Do it on the cell phone, in person, hell, even by notes if you have to to get the conversation started. Do whatever it takes to get the job done!

Communication

Ah, the bane of the parent-teenager relationship for millennia. Everybody knows how hard it is to communicate with your children. And trying to communicate in a world of LOL, TTFN, LABFLWAO, and BFF can make it even harder. Society at large is not much help with its ever-changing motif and liberalism.

But, despite the cliché, it is absolutely imperative that you be able to communicate with your teenager, probably more so now than ever—although parents have said the same thing for ages!

If you've encouraged communication with your children since they were small, it should be easier. But lots of things change as the hormones inside those bodies start surging.

As parents, we believe that our precious darlings will always be ten years old, so innocent, patiently listening to our every utterance, waiting for our kernels of wisdom to come out and brighten their day. They sit wide-eyed and awestruck as you gently instruct them on handling life's problems and determining how they fit into the world. Wait—I'm sorry. That was on the Disney Channel; it's not reality but the stuff of dreamland.

In the real world, kids have always rolled their eyes at us, and usually what we try to tell them goes in one ear and out the other. We embarrass and humiliate them by being so attentive and worried about their safety. And our admonitions to be good and stay out of trouble are usually met with a sarcastic, "Yes, Dad. Can I go now?"

But deep down, most teenagers—I'd venture to say 90 percent—are happy to hear that we care and love them enough to cause them such embarrassment and humiliation in front of their friends. When my son was still a teen, I heard his friends say several times, "I wish my dad would say that junk, but he's never home." It warms a doddering old man's heart to hear such things.

Talk to your children incessantly, even when they want to scream because you're talking too much. Talk about anything until you hit a subject they have wondered about, and you'll be able to tell by the quizzical look on their face.

When they say they don't want to talk, give them some room to think, but don't let them brood by themselves for too long. Knock on their door and go in and start talking. About what you ask. Bring up all those horrible (or wonderful) memories that you have of being a teenager. Relate the embarrassments in your life.

If you know your child as well as you should, most of the time you'll have a good sense of what's eating at them. At the point that you isolate the one or ten things wrong, you can talk intelligently about them. But don't offer ironclad solutions. That's the last thing most teenagers want. Give them your view, tell how you handled it as a teen, and then leave them alone.

In today's world, it can be close to impossible to have a coherent conversation with your children. But you have to try to *do whatever it takes to get the job done right!*

You may have seen the commercial about talking to your kids about drugs, where the parent leaves sticky notes everywhere. Take the same approach. Leave them sticky notes saying that you want to talk. Keep doing it until you get the response you want.

There are many other ways to talk to your teenager. With modern conveniences, we can easily converse with anyone across the world. Text them, send them an e-mail or instant message; leave a voice mail—whatever it takes.

And last, there are always two reliable "old-timer favorites"—having dinner together (or some daily meal) and playing catch in the backyard. I know it sounds kind of *Leave It to Beaver*ish, but it works.

With your sons, you can play catch in the backyard so you won't embarrass them by talking where "everyone" can see. As for your daughters, take them shopping or to dinner. You do whatever it takes to have some one-on-one time for the two of you.

As for dinner, it's hard to sit next to or across from someone and not talk. The subject matter doesn't matter at all.

Does being the rigid, stick-in-the-mud parent make you popular with your children? Probably not, at least on the outside but in the long run, it could pay many more dividends than you can imagine.

Lawsuits

We live in a society that has gone mad with suing one another for stupid, little reasons, like "I got my feelings hurt," "I didn't get what I wanted," or "I don't like that thing there." And the list goes on.

Our lenient society—looking for equality for everyone and everything—coupled with trial lawyers making a bundle, makes the idea of making easy money off an organization with deep pockets hard to resist. But is it worth it? Ponder that—is it really worth it?

A woman sued McDonald's because her coffee was too hot and she spilled it in her lap while driving her car, and she was awarded hundreds of thousands of dollars for her own stupidity. Another woman sued a restaurant because she slipped on the water on the floor, which was only there because she threw her glass of water into the face of her boyfriend. No one wants to take responsibility for their own actions. And if we as adults can't take responsibility, then how can we expect our kids to take it?

In reality, who pays for these lawsuits? Certainly not the organizations being sued! If it's a public company like McDonald's, then consumers pay for it because they'll just raise prices. If it's a nonprofit, then we all still pay in reduced services and assistance in the community.

Have you wondered why our kids can't play tag, dodge ball, or other such children's games anymore at school? Most of the time, it's because the school administration is afraid of the liability that comes with little Susie falling down and skinning her knee.

We as parents want to wrap our kids up in bubble wrap so they won't get hurt. But we live in dangerous world, and there are more important things to worry about than a skinned knee. Kids are kids. They fall down and go boom; that's what kids do. Should parents be prosecuted because a child breaks an arm by tripping over a garden hose in the front yard?

Not everything that happens to us in life is fair or compensatory. If it was an honest mistake, then let it go and learn from it. Just like in the real world, we can't sue over hot coffee when that's what we ordered.

Last, let me offer just a little food for thought: letting our kids run around and play aggressively on the playground helps them to cope. Our children are growing up without coping mechanisms for stress and anger. If we let them blow off steam at recess or in physical education class, we could be helping ourselves in the long run.

And if children fall down and injure themselves, we have to think, "Did they get thrown or pushed down with malice, or was it just youthful exuberance? Did they bruise their knees, or did they break a bone?" In either incident, teach from it—it's okay to play rough if you're just playing. Hurting someone for malicious reasons is wrong.

Not every slight or injury is avoidable, nor should they be compensated for. When we as parents sue for silly little reasons, we all lose.

It Takes a Village

What I am talking about is going back in time to the days when families were still families and we looked after and took care of one another—a time that now seems foreign to most parents and especially our kids.

When I was a child, everybody on the block watched out for me. If I did something wrong, my grandparents knew about it before I could walk back home! If I did something right, they also found out about it quickly. The people on the block took care of all the kids that lived there.

When I was about nine, a family moved in next door. The twin boys were constantly doing things to get into trouble. When the parents were informed by the neighborhood network, they denied it was their boys, said everyone was mistaken, and then screamed that their sons would never do anything like that.

There are too many parents today who are unwilling to listen to the tales of the mischief their kids make. When informed of these things, like my new neighbors, they scream, threaten, and belittle the informer, who has done nothing except tell them that their little darling broke a bottle on the sidewalk down the street.

As parents and neighbors, we need to go back to the days when we looked out for one another and one another's kids. The most unneighborly thing we can do is verbally assault the kindly, caring person informing us. If we verbally assault or ridicule our neighbor for doing that, then what are we teaching our children? The simple answer is that by shouting someone down and making them feel guilty, you can get away with things anywhere, anytime—even at school.

As responsible parents, we need to accept the information and thank our neighbor. Am I saying that all complaining neighbors are looking after the welfare of our children? Absolutely not, there are some curmudgeons who will complain about anything and everything, and you always have to take their complaints with a grain of salt.

While it is good to defend your children against unfounded accusations, we must be realistic and listen to a whole neighborhood. Too often today, parents are unrealistic. Remember; where there is smoke, there is fire. I'm not saying you should blindly accept everything your neighbors tell you about your children, but don't blindly refuse to acknowledge the possibility that some of what you hear could be true.

We need to *all* work together to raise our kids in an environment of caring and tolerance. Teaching the difference between right and wrong is not a job only for the parents. It is the job of everyone our children come into contact with, and that means even the cashier at the corner store.

Verbally assaulting, ridiculing, or physically assaulting someone does nothing but send the wrong message to our children. And ponder this: do we get so defensive because we know that we are lacking in parenting skills and can't control our children?

Spying

Many parents will balk at this one area of responsibility even if they accept everything else written here. And the reasoning is simple: it goes against the grain that you trust your teenager. The KGB went out with the eighties.

I agree that no one should be spied on without good reason. However, teenagers are not just any people. Sometimes they need to be watched like a hawk, and sometimes their rooms need to be searched.

If the parents of Dylan Klebold and Eric Harris had been more suspicious and done a better job of spying, maybe there wouldn't have been a Columbine massacre.

So, you ask, when should you search your teenager's room? Anytime that something doesn't seem quite right or you suspect something? I'll tell you, I've not a clue. As a parent, no one should know your child better than you, so only you would know when this is needed.

What should you be looking for? That's a little easier for me to answer. If you're doing a physical search, then obviously it would be anything inappropriate—pornography, cigarettes, drugs, alcohol, firearms, and banned (from your house) videos and music, for starters. Where you look is just as important as what you look for. If you suspect your child is using drugs, then a hard search of every book, CD case, etc., should be considered. I have heard of private companies in some cities and states renting out retired drug-sniffing dogs for a visit to your home.

Aside from those types of items, you need to search their computers, especially if you've allowed unrestricted Internet access in their rooms. There are many ways to check on what your teens have been looking at or searching for on the World Wide Web. Set passwords so you can access their files on their computers. Check their rooms for unauthorized software such as hacking software or anti-spyware. Check their Internet logs, and set them up so they cannot be erased.

Looking at the cookie cache is one way to see what sites have been visited. Cookies are parcels of text that Web sites can place on your hard drive to allow for easier access, to spy on search habits, and so on. Most are innocuous, but they can be very informative for a concerned parent.

Another way is to look at their Internet tracks. Every time they look at a Web site, the computer saves some information about it. It doesn't save more than a few at a time, but it will show you the last few sites they visited. In 1996, there was only one Web site that promoted hate against a group of people; in 2008, there were more than 100,000. That is reason enough to check up on what kids are taking in.

Another option is available if you believe trouble is brewing, and by that I mean you fear that your teenager daughter is discussing sex and considering running away with an older man, planning a Columbine-style attack, dealing or abusing drugs, or engaging in any other nefarious type of cyber talk. You can install a keystroke program. This will allow you to track everything your teen does while online. It records every key stroke that she makes and saves it in a file for you to retrieve later. This will let you see exactly what she is saying, planning, and doing online, including all the Web sites she visits.

While you need to allow some privacy for your teenagers, you need to remember several points:

1) They live in your house, and you are responsible for them.
2) You own the house and everything in it; even if you are only renting, you are still paying the rent.
3) Until they are eighteen years old, you are emotionally, physically, and financially responsible for them. So you're not only protecting them from potentially dangerous things but also protecting your own keister.

If you have a "good" kid, then you shouldn't have to spend much time in their rooms. Unfortunately, the world is littered with the bodies of the victims of "good kids" whose parents were too busy or too trusting of their little angels.

Teenagers are secretive and want their privacy. It's only natural; they are growing into adults and trying to find out who they are. But whether they know it or not, they need your help to do that, and they need guidance in stopping drug abuse, murder, hate speech, or other such things.

Snitching

I know, I know. No one likes a tattletale. But there are a time when snitching is the right thing to do. Unfortunately, most parents don't like snitches, kids are awfully hard on tattletales, and much of the time the person who's snitching has a self-esteem or confidence problem.

What we have to do is instruct our children on when it is okay to tattle on someone. As parents and school administrators, we frequently tell our kids that it's wrong to tattle on someone else. But instead of making blanket statements that being a tattletale is wrong, we need to tell them the difference between proper "snitching" and just being a plain tattletale. So what is the difference between a tattletale and a proper snitch? I'm glad you asked.

A tattletale will inform any adult in a position of authority something just to get someone in trouble or to curry favor with the adult. We all experienced that in grade school. And unfortunately, sometimes it continues into our workplaces with backstabbing and office politics. Sound familiar?

On the other hand, proper snitching is done for the good of the one being informed on. The informers don't do it for personal or selfish reasons, per se. They do it for the safety of the individual or group that they're telling on.

Here are two examples of what I mean.

Ten-year-old Susie doesn't like Tommy because he teases her in all those ways that ten-year-old boys tease little girls. Tommy likes taking a shortcut behind the school to go home, where he likes to throw rocks at old billboards. There is no real safety issue, but it's private property and the old man who owns it is grumpy about it. With her naturally curly hair and doe eyes, Susie tells the teacher, Tommy has to take a note home, and Susie gets the satisfaction of having an adult on her side and Tommy humiliated.

The following incident actually occurred in April 2006. The names of the students, high school, & city have been changed by request of all involved; It was a bright spring day in Devils Lake. 17 year old Steve was reveling in the fact that in a month he would be graduating and be free to change the world. Little did he know he would change it starting today instead. Steve's best friend since 1st grade was Jimmy. Jimmy had been having a problem with another senior in school. The druggie and Jimmy had gone at it more than once, some on campus some off. Jimmy was tired of being a tackling dummy to this guy.

No matter how much Steve tried to help, Jimmy was bullheaded and stubborn. He insisted that no one help even when he got his butt kicked. That bright spring day after school, Jimmy told Steve that he was going to take care of the problem once and for all the next day with his shotgun. Steve was startled and frightened by those words.

He wrangled all night with his conundrum. He hemmed and hawed and beat the bushes about asking his parents. Finally, his decision was made. He told his parents, who contacted the school, who in turn notified the police.

Jimmy was stopped the next morning as he left his driveway. A loaded 12 gauge shotgun was found in his car and he was arrested. Subsequently Jimmy was expelled from school and missed graduating with his class. And while that was bad, Steve felt like he got the worst of it. He was ostracized from his friends, class, & the school. He even received threats on his life for 'snitching'. He received his diploma in a private ceremony and went to college depressed at losing his friends.

Steve later talked to the media and other students at the high school. 'I felt bad for doing it, I mean Jimmy had been my best friend for almost my whole life, But I would have felt even guiltier if I hadn't said something and someone would have gotten hurt, even a person like the bully'.

Now do you see the difference? We can no longer accept our kids' keeping their mouths shut when someone might be in danger, and we can no longer tell our kids that snitching is wrong. If you snitch and save a life, even if it's the life of someone you don't like, isn't it worth the risk?

The Gadgets

Ah, the gadgets that come with being a teenager— cell phones, iPods, computers, video game systems. Hell, teenagers need only depart their rooms to forage for food and go to school, especially if they have their own bathrooms! That's the way for a teenager to live.

"Buzz" goes the game show buzzer. Wrong answer, but thank you very much for playing. You'll get a reality check as a door prize. And here it is.

Teenagers should never be allowed to have all of those toys in their rooms, especially if they're unsupervised. I am not against teenagers' having some toys, but not to the degree that some parents go and teenagers want.

Let me explain what I feel is acceptable and what isn't.

Having a computer in their rooms is not a bad idea. They can do their homework and study. But it shouldn't have Internet access or a private printer. Nor should you allow discs from other computers to be uploaded into the system; many vile things can be hidden on them. While on the subject, let me offer a word of caution about buying used computers. A friend bought his family a used computer and took it to the computer store to have it wiped clean and everything reinstalled. Well, there was a back-up drive that no one found except their precocious child. It was filled with images of child pornography.

As for television sets, DVD or video players, and game systems, again, these items are not bad in and of themselves. But they should not have cable or satellite hookups. If you allowed the cable hookups, you'd spend months blocking channels. Videos and game systems are okay for them to have, but what goes into them is what is suspect. We'll get into appropriate entertainment in a few pages, but suffice it to say that what they view or play has to be censored.

Radios should be allowed, but I would draw the line at large stereo systems. For a teenager to have a stereo system is completely inappropriate, although it is a teenager's dream. It is just another toy in their room that separates them from the family. Able to shut out siblings and parents with relative ease. Another distraction from homework and their responsibilities. And besides, if there is a need to take away this toy as well for punishment who in the world wants to deal with all that spaghetti (wires) more than once. A small boom box with a tape/CD player is also okay, as are portable players such as MP3 players. The argument is about what is played on them.

Cell phones are one item that I am against teenagers having. If it is a limited-scope phone that only a limited number of other, selected numbers can reach and that is programmed with emergency numbers for your family and 9-1-1, it's fine. But allowing teenagers to have unlimited access to the Internet and texting in their hands is a disaster waiting to happen.

While the concept of owning a cell phone is perfectly acceptable, teenagers do not need to have all of the bells and whistles. If you don't allow them to access the Internet in their rooms, why would you allow it everywhere else unmonitored?

Now comes the nightmare of all teenagers: crime and punishment. If your teenagers are being punished (grounded) for an infraction, why then would you send them to toy land? If you are going to allow them to have gadgets in their rooms, then you must also have a way to take them away.

Most kids would love to be sent to their rooms and grounded if they have all those toys. Take them away if necessary. Having those toys in their rooms is a *privilege,* not a right. Confiscate the TV, DVD player, game system, stereo, cell phone, and whatever else.

Now the inevitable question—what if they get a job and buy the toys themselves? The answer is that if you are against them buying it and don't want them to have it, then don't let them get it. If you allow them to buy it, then make the stipulation that, at your discretion, it can be confiscated at any time.

Entertainment

So much has been made of how bad the entertainment industry is, and I agree with most of the criticism. The entertainment industry as a whole is to blame for what it produces.

The movies being released push political agendas, not to mention sex, violence, and other things. What is considered appropriate for a thirteen-year-old now would have been rated R in the seventies, and it's not because we have evolved to a higher sense of freedom.

The same goes for most rap music. As many of my younger friends say, the music of the seventies and eighties was just as bad, they just weren't as free to express it in a profane way. In some ways I do agree with that, but as a man far wiser than me once said, "Just because we can do a thing doesn't mean we should."

Songs about sex have been around forever, but they used to be more subtle. These days, they're much more direct. I'll quote from a song I heard during a "concert" at a stop light: "Fuck that nigger ho, she's got fuckin' pussy and I gotta snag that bitch." Excuse my language, but why do we need that?

Then there are the video games. From sports games such as NFL Blitz to Grand Theft Auto, even our video games are overly violent. If you're not familiar with these, let me explain. NFL Blitz is a football game that encourages players to commit dirty play. What would get a player ejected and suspended from the actual NFL is acceptable and even encouraged. Maybe I'm a purist, but I don't think that teaches good sportsmanlike behavior or how to act in real life.

Grand Theft Auto is a game in which the player gets points by stealing cars, killing drug dealers, selling drugs, killing cops, and having sex. I tell ya, that's a wholesome way of teaching teenagers about dealing with life and authority—not.

But is anything wrong with these forms of entertainment? Fundamentally, no. But over a period of time, what starts as something unique and new turns into normality. How do you think China, Russia, and other communist countries are able to hold power for so long? They repeatedly tell the populace what is good for them, even if common sense says otherwise, until it is the norm. It's called brainwashing.

Now the question is who is to blame? The answer that everyone wants to give is the entertainment industry. But is that fair? After all, they're only doing what they're supposed to—fulfilling a need. So if we can't blame them, then who? How about the government? They need to tighten controls on who can buy what where. But do we really want the government intruding into our lives even more?

The answer is as simple as looking in the mirror. What? That's right, we as parents, grandparents, guardians, teachers, and society in general are responsible. As with other points in this book, it is not hard to explain.

We as parents and guardians allow the videos, movies, games, and music into our homes. We allow our teenagers to listen to, play, and watch these things. Who buys our teenagers these things without looking at the packaging simply because they can't live without it? We do.

We allow all of these things in our homes, cars, schools, and other places where our kids congregate. So it is up to us to stop them from listening, watching, and playing. If it doesn't come into our homes, then it can't brainwash our kids. Some say, "But they can always get it at a friend's house." This may be true, but remember that as a parent, it's your responsibility to know who your teens are associating with. If you don't like what others are allowing in their homes, then you don't allow the association.

I had this battle with my son. He brought home several CDs that had very explicit lyrics. I forbade him from having them in the house, and I also grounded him from his best friend's house because the friend listened to such music. I said that his friend could come to our house anytime. This worked well until my ex-wife undermined the whole process – one reason she's an ex.

Letting the Child Fail

You may think that this is a preposterous idea. Letting children fail? That's just not fair. It'll hurt their self-esteem. They'll grow up to be too competitive. They won't have respect for others. They can't … STOP ALREADY!

I am sick to death of schools that propagate the idea that every child is equal. They are not! This is just another way to make everyone feel good. Grading on a curve, not keeping score, and giving everyone a trophy just don't happen in the real world.

The only valid argument that I can agree with is that kids are kids for only so long. So, we should let them have as happy and carefree a life as they can now before things get really hard. Well, that statement is only slightly less ludicrous than most of the others for this type of antifailure mentality present in our schools and society.

Kids need to be taught that failure is something that occurs in everyday life. When they get into the real world, there will be no do-overs. There is no rule that everyone is equal; if that were true, we'd all be doctors or hamburger flippers at the local burger joint.

Educators and parents need to offer children the chance for the learning and growing that happens when they fail. It is a learning tool. Instruct them on why it's not a bad thing to fail and that the world will not come to an end because they failed.

Failure isn't something to shy away from. Learning that failure is part of life better prepares our kids for those challenging teenager years ahead, when they'll need to know how to handle failure on a daily basis.

When babies grow and start to walk, they fall down a lot. What do we tell them? "Oh my sweetums, it's okay. Just get up and keep trying and you'll get it!" And when they master walking, we tell them what? "Oh pumpkin, I am so proud of you. You learned to walk!" And the beaming smile you get from their victory is overwhelming.

Most of us, at least on the playground, forgot about the score of the kickball game as soon as the class bell rang. And as for competitive sports, children are incredibly good at moving on after losing a game. They don't need adults mucking it up with the entire self-esteem talk. Eventually, they'll view the trophy they got for finishing last as stupid and foolish.

By allowing our kids to fail now, we teach them how to handle failure later. If we teach them early and often, they will at least know what to expect later, and maybe they won't have the frustration, depression, and anxiety when they move into their teenage years.

Picking Your Battles, by Eileen

Many parents try to micromanage their children from an early age. That's okay if it works for you. As for me, I decided I wanted my children to be more independent and self-aware, so I gave them choices at a very early age—not all the choices, but one or two. When my son reached the age of two, I realized I had given birth to a royal handful, probably because my mother once wished upon me, "I hope you have a child just like you." I was not going to win every battle with him; heck, I wasn't sure I would even win the war. So I sat down and imagined what his teenage years would be like and rethought my current strategy. I decided on which battles were going to be worth going full bore and which ones could be open for negotiation. By deciding not to fight about everything and being open to discussion, I chose to be open and honest with my child. Perish the thought I would let my son run wild, but I remember my teenage years as the time I developed my own sense of worth and identity. My parents, having instilled a very strong sense of right and wrong within me, let me explore the many different identities I may have wanted when I grew up. So while I had a very strict set of boundaries to live within, I also had the freedom to explore who I might want to be. Because my son was as strong-minded and pigheaded as me, I knew it was going to be a long, long, long stretch of years. I had three major battles I was willing to wage. They were school, drinking, and drugs.

School: Good grades and good attendance were my battles. My son needed to learn that doing his homework and projects was his responsibility, not mine or the teacher's. When he was in seventh grade, I stepped back and let him take the lead on doing his homework and school projects, reminding him once a day to do his homework. He decided to goof off and ended up almost flunking seventh grade. I was okay with his suffering the consequences of his actions. His father was on the other side of the street and felt he needed to be badgered every evening to do his homework and rode as hard as a bucking bronco till it was completed. Yep, it was certainly a character-building exercise … for Dad, not for teen.

Drugs/alcohol: Lucky for me, I didn't have any problems with my son in this area. Having had open and honest discussions with him about drugs and alcohol throughout his years until he reached the age of peer pressure and experimentation, we had already established the base. My son and I had an open line of communication between us, so I never worried about it. Okay, I was naive, but I survived.

Clothing: The majority of teens discover Goth around seventh or eighth grade, and my son was no exception. My ex wanted "his" son to reflect "his" sense of style and "his" sense of self-worth, but my teen wanted to wear only black or dark colors. My only insistence was his clothes be clean and that he shower daily—basically, keep up his personal hygiene. Otherwise, he was free to express his own point of view. This battle wasn't one of my high priorities. He knew that when we went out as a family, I preferred that he wear something less somber, and he usually complied unless we were going someplace his friends from school might be.

Hair: I liked for my son's hair to be clean and well-groomed, but I didn't care about length or style. I figured it was just hair and would grow. It is an expression of who they are thinking about being, not the image of who they will be the rest of their lives.

Friends: Again, I knew who his friends were, where they hung out, and when he was going to be home. He had strict boundaries, but the rules were flexible within those boundaries. I didn't want him having friends who did drugs or were part of gangs, but living in North Idaho, I didn't have to worry much about that in the nineties.

Really, the point to all of this is that you need to figure out what is important to you and what you can let slide a bit. Your children grow up part mom, part dad, part grandparents, and mostly themselves, who they are comfortable with deep inside. You guide them and support them, but it still is their journey of discovery and you can't do it for them. Start them young, teaching them right from wrong and all the values you hold dear. Just remember that they will choose the ones they'll live by, not you.

School Accountability

All of the blame can't be laid at the feet of the parents. Our schools in recent years have tried to become parents, and that just doesn't work. The administrators, with their time invested in doctorate degrees, think of new programs that are doomed to fail or boondoggle. An overabundance of touchy-feely self-esteem–building programs are flooding the schools, as well as other things that I don't have much respect for, such as no recess or recess with only "nice" games.

One way that schools allow violence in is by denying that they have a problem. In many schools, the crime rate is grossly underreported. One school in Pennsylvania reported over 800 criminal activities, but an audit revealed that it actually had over 3,500 incidents! The school was ordered to reorganize its system to reflect the results of the audit. School officials have been notorious for not reporting assaults for fear of losing their positions.

Increasingly, we are finding sexual assault as well. Weapons are found on almost a daily basis. Even in rural schools, we're finding "hit lists."

Our schools need be held accountable for not reporting problems and putting our children in danger. One event in Arizona illustrates this.

A student's mother found a hit list in her son's backpack. She immediately took the list and her son to the school principal's office. In order not to alarm the school, and in violation of district procedures, the principal let the matter drop because the mother and son promised to get counseling. A week later, the boy was arrested for having a serrated steak knife with him at school.

Again, and I will refer to this very often, COMMUNICATION between parents, schools, and students is absolutely vital in keeping anything more than fistfights out of the school. We have to talk to one another in order to know what is going on inside the school and the student body.

As a side note to parents, teachers, and students, I want to say that if someone comes to you and reports a weapon or that they suspect something is about to happen, listen to them. Some people may call it snitching, but I call it courage when you risk the disapproval of your peers to satisfy your conscience. Never dismiss a threat or even a rumor of a threat, and don't forget that your child's friends and your child are never above suspicion.

Communication

One of the things I will harp on throughout this book is communication. A philosophy of effective communication is needed just as much at the school level as anywhere, and maybe more so. Schools are the place where kids are supposed to be learning to communicate, and many times they won't learn by observing.

In most schools, the unspoken policy is "Tell us all you know, and we'll tell you nothing." The administrators will tell you to inform them of problems or potential problems, and then instead of passing it along to someone who might be better able to handle it, they conveniently "forget" and file it away. Not all administrators are that way—some are enlightened enough to try to get something done—but just as often they are blocked at the district level.

The same is true for other school personnel, such as secretaries who don't, or won't, pass along messages to those who make decisions and teachers and counselors who believe they know better than anyone and don't talk with other administrators. Making it worse are the schools that refuse to talk with students and parents simply because they don't have to.

The lack of transparency at most school districts is appalling. They make decisions concerning our kids but never explain them adequately to parents or students, and sometimes not even very well to staff. It's often like trying to get a straight answer from a politician. Many times I have found myself in a shell game with administrators, leaving with more questions than I came with.

The school's responsibility is to recognize that students, and by extension their parents, are the most important things in the school. If an issue involves more than procedural changes in the office, then students and parents need to be informed.

Likewise, if a parent or concerned citizen calls the school and leaves a message, then it should be returned promptly, no matter how stupid or trivial the school thinks it is. It's important to someone or they wouldn't have called. As I ask people in my customer service classes, how long does it take to return a phone call? The parents' perception of the teachers, administrators, counselors, and others would improve overnight if they took a few minutes to call back.

There are absolutely no excuses for not returning phone calls to parents or others—even salespeople. When I was in school and when my youngest went to school, it was not uncommon to receive a phone call from a teacher as late as 9:00 p.m. to discuss a potential problem. Fortunately, neither my grandparents nor I received many of those calls. But in many instances, teachers are disciplined for not taking the issue to administration first, where it can be conveniently buried in a file and the teacher possibly disciplined for raising the issue and threatening the administrators' bonuses.

Do parents and students need to be told everything? No. For example, the school should inform parents if cameras are being installed, but in the interest of security, the locations should be kept quiet and the installation completed at night or on weekends.

Communication between parents and children is of paramount importance, but communication between the school and parents is equally important, as well as between the school and the students. Information works best if it flows freely; therefore, parents, students, and others also need to communicate with the school.

One way to do that, which we'll discuss later, is holding quarterly or monthly informational meetings with parents to discuss overall issues. They should be run much like a city council meeting, with representatives from the district, school board, students, parents, and school administration present.

Lawsuits

As I stated before, our society is too litigious. We sue each other and companies for every *perceived* wrong. But who is that helping? Is it helping the educational process to sue our schools?

The answer to that is a simple NO! Any time a group or individual sues a school, district, or administrator, it hurts all of us but our children most of all.

Even if the lawsuit is dropped, the school will have spent money to defend itself. Furthermore, there are the costs of questioning witnesses, gathering evidence, using court time, and losing time in the classroom. Eventually, these are absorbed by the school and passed along to the students in the form of budget cuts, eliminated programs, cancelled field trips, and the inability to purchase new materials.

The potential of being sued has school teachers, administrators, and districts walking on eggshells. They are scared to do what needs to be done or to let the children be children. Then they are worried about their own job security should anything happen.

Allowing kids to be kids and release their energy, stress, and aggression out on the playground is gone. We are so worried that we will get sued because little Susie fell down and skinned her knee or that Jimmy caused Timmy to feel bad because he tagged him. How is that fair?

Some parents have questioned fairness when suing a school over some perceived slight, but let me turn that around. How is it fair to the other kids that their playtime is as restricted as that in a prison recreation yard? The answer is that it's not.

School administrators need to do the right thing and allow kids to play and act like kids before they get older. A line in John Cougar Mellencamp's song "Jack and Diane" is apropos: "Hold on to sixteen as long as you can. Changes come around real soon and make us women and men."

If we allow kids in the lower grades (K–6) to have a normal recess, they will learn more about handling stress and negative feelings than a whole lifetime full of counselors could provide. By letting them be kids, they'll learn how to fail and how to keep trying, and they will direct their energy and aggressive tendencies in a positive manner without even knowing it.

So we can't be afraid to let kids play and get hurt, but we also have to realize that there are other things that we can be sued over that can't be avoided.

As a case in point, schools have switched from the term "Christmas break" to "winter vacation." Why? Because they were threatened with a lawsuit if they didn't include everyone. Let's be realistic: not everyone is equal! We are all different. We all have different beliefs. But we take a vacation during Christmas.

Teachers, administrators, and district bureaucrats, listen up. Don't do the politically correct thing or even the safe thing. Do what's right for the kids. That is, after all, why we're here, isn't it?

It Takes a Village

This is yet another of the things I will harp on throughout this book, but this time the context is a bit different than what was discussed regarding parental responsibility. This is the village you entrust your child to for seven hours a day.

While the arena may be different, the content is essentially the same. Teachers, counselors, administrators, and security or resource officers must all work together in order to protect our kids while they're at school, which is supposedly the safest place away from home—at least it should be.

These people need to talk with one another and spread their knowledge of the system to the newbies. But beyond that, they need to pass along tips to one another about potential problem students, instead of just leaving it to administration.

Without fear of being bullied and harassed by administrators (thereby creating a *workplace* violence situation in the school), they need to be able to discuss students amongst themselves, conveying their fears, troubles, and experiences to one another.

Oftentimes these issues will get swept under the rug and dismissed as paranoia. As with parents, a quarterly or monthly (I would prefer monthly) meeting just for teachers, counselors, and others to discuss problem students and what their issues are would be helpful. As these meetings progress, a "warning signs" list may need to be compiled and, if necessary, the parents contacted.

The full staff at the school needs to be involved in instructing teenagers and in keeping them safe, including the security guards or resource officers (the difference being the certification to carry a firearm and arrest powers), teachers, counselors, and administrators, as well as everyone in between. Even the janitors can contribute to raising our teens.

The school, then, has an obligation to inform parents or others if a situation warrants. Teachers shouldn't be afraid to send home a note or call the parents with bad news. We have to put the days of not taking responsibility behind us. Many times, teachers are the target of some of the most bellicose barrel of bull I've ever heard, all from parents who blame everyone except their little angels and themselves.

Ponder this point: if you could stop a Columbine-style massacre by making one little phone call, would you? Many at Columbine wish they had had some information compiled before April 20, 1999.

Zero Tolerance

I would be willing to bet you a million bucks that most schools in this country have a policy on zero tolerance. And under those policies, I could be expelled, suspended, or placed into a level-five detention for what I just said. Huh?

You see, nearly all zero-tolerance policies draw absolutely no distinctions. I might be making a joke about gambling, as in the above paragraph, but to administrators in most states, I just committed a felony.

You might say that making jokes about betting and making jokes about guns and drugs are different. In practice, no, they aren't. What makes any of these comments dangerous is the context in which they're taken.

This section is more on common sense in applying the policy rather than the policy itself. I fully believe in a zero-tolerance policy, but come on, knuckleheads, use some common sense!

For example, a girl is making her bologna, cheese, and ketchup sandwich for lunch (using ketchup on bologna is a crime in my book, anyway), and she hears the school bus grinding and belching smoke down the street. She throws her lunch into the bag and takes off running. Later, she's expelled for bringing a weapon to school. This is after she discovers she threw the butter knife in with her lunch and takes it to the office because she knows she shouldn't have it and tries to explain what happened.

I have hundreds of stories like this, and many do not involve weapons. How about the girl who shares a Tylenol with her best friend and gets suspended for dealing drugs, or the fifth-grader who was expelled for completing an art assignment to make a scary Halloween mask that someone *thought* might have a gang-related symbol on it?

The problem is that too many teachers and administrators have a knee-jerk reaction to these types of actions or comments. Do I agree that suspending or expelling a student for these actions is appropriate? Absolutely—sometimes.

If the dunderheads would have taken the time to know their students and investigate, they would have discovered that none of the above students showed any of the other signs of someone about to commit violence, nor were they in any other at-risk group.

The same goes for threats. Know when teens are joking. There is a difference between grumbling about losing the big game and joking about blowing their friends' brains out. How do we know these things? By the school doing its job to investigate and solve it quickly, not days later.

I guess the point I'm trying to make is that while zero-tolerance policies are good and wonderful things, they can turn an already autocratic system into Russia under Stalin or Germany under Hitler, where someone is guilty until proven innocent. But then people are still guilty because they broke the "spirit" of the policy. It's the gulag for them.

Chapter 3

Factors That Can Actually Promote Violence

While we all agree that something has to be done to stop violence against our teens, there is another side of us that actually promotes violence. And I don't mean just the schools or other students. Good parents are just as much at fault as those parents who don't care.

Parents who couldn't care less about their kids no matter what they do can be a problem. However, those parents who adopt a very strict disciplinary style with their children can be at fault. Once again, I've got you scratching your noggin.

As you will see in the following pages, not everyone falls into neat groups. There are many facets to unwittingly promoting violence against another, but you have to have an open mind.

Most of the items in this section will be laid at the feet of schools. But many parents can also be blamed for such things as CHH, NIH (both defined later), stereotyping, and perceptions. Many times, both parents do it without thinking about it.

Strict, disciplinary schools and homes are fine and sometimes needed, but there has to be a relative atmosphere of open-mindedness. Your mind doesn't have to be closed to ideas if you're strict—even if you create a boot camp setting or are deeply religious.

You may be surprised and maybe even upset at some of the things I'll say in the following pages.

NIH

I know what you're thinking: "Oh geez, another acronym. Just what I needed—more alphabet soup." Well, this one is different. It could save the life of your child.

NIH stands for "not invented here." What does that mean? You ask. The basic meaning is that we don't listen to any new ideas from anyone outside our homes—and even that is limited to one person in many cases.

While there is nothing wrong with a strict matriarchal or patriarchal household, such arrangements can cause more divisions than seamless family life. The same goes for schools.

In nearly all businesses, there is a level of trust and understanding that employees can offer suggestions. Why should teenagers be treated any different in that respect? Granted, their suggestions may not be based in reality, but neither are many proposed by adults. The key is that you allow the suggestion to be heard.

Teenagers are the next generation. They have to be able to make decisions and suggestions in order to improve their critical thinking skills.

And even when you get a suggestion that seems frivolous, you can't just dismiss it out of hand and you can't ridicule it either. Doing so does nothing more than humiliate the child, whether we as adults think so or not.

Schools and school districts are the biggest offenders in this area after parents. Our kids have better success at making suggestions for improvement at the local burger joint than at home or school.

As adults, we don't just dismiss a co-worker's or colleague's suggestions outright. We at least give some thought to the idea. It may not be a good one, but we at least listen.

The same should be done for kids. If their suggestion is sound but unworkable at the time, tell them that and why it's unworkable. I've heard too many parents and teachers say, "That's the dumbest idea yet. We can't do that!"

I have just as often heard the sorry, tired excuse that we've never done that before, or worse, that we've always done it this way and it works. Follow the advice I give to my business clients, which is also the title of my favorite book: if it ain't broke, break it!

Just because we're adults doesn't mean that we have cornered the market on good ideas. Our kids have wonderful ideas, and if we give them the chance, they might make better suggestions or solve problems we didn't see. Maybe we can help them to become adults with open minds who employ critical thinking.

CHH

Yeah, I know—yet another set of letters as an acronym. This one can also be termed in a less flattering set of words: the Ostrich Syndrome.

Now you're asking what six-foot-tall, flightless birds have to do with school violence. It's all apparent in the words behind the acronym. CHH means "can't happen here."

This is the most maddening attitude to me in the world. "We have such good kids in our school, nothing like that could ever happen here." I have heard this excuse from school districts that have problems but that also have administrators who are too blind to see them.

And it's not just limited to schools and teachers. Parents are just as likely to stick their heads in the sand, maybe more so. Their little angels would never be close to anything like that.

Schools, parents, and society at large ignore the problems and think they'll go away. The U.S. Postal Service thought the same way about violent incidents in the 1980s, and we all know what happened. A new phrase was added to the vernacular—going postal.

We think that if we don't talk about the problem, it won't be there when we open our eyes or that if we just spend more money on studying the problem, it'll go away. Or maybe if we spend money on training for what to do *after* an incident, it'll help.

I can tell you flat out what those things will do for our children. Programs will be cut because we spent hundreds of thousands of dollars on consultants, studies, or training. Or the school administrators will say they'll look into a solution. Or worse yet, the government will get involved because no one wants to take responsibility.

The end result will be the same no matter the proposed solution. We'll have our children being assaulted or murdered at school. That's not a pleasant thought, is it?

Parents, you need to know that your school district is a governmental agency. It receives your tax dollars to operate. Therefore, it is up to you to ensure that proper methods are implemented to keep your kids safe.

Playing ostrich doesn't work when you're two and playing peek-a-boo, and it doesn't work for adults. The problem of school violence has to be confronted and dealt with. It doesn't have to happen in the media, but it will not get any better if we sit in closed rooms, wringing our hands and saying there is nothing we can do.

Communication

When I started writing this book, I didn't give much thought to communication. But as the outline progressed into what you are now reading, it became clear that communication plays such a vital role in so many aspects of the school violence problem.

I won't spend a lot of time on it here; I discuss it in detail elsewhere. But let me say these few things and reiterate my points on the subject.

Communication between everyone involved with our teenagers is vital—not just between them and their parents. Communication is needed between everyone.

Schools need to be more transparent in communicating with teachers, parents, and teenagers. Teachers need to be unafraid of retribution so they can communicate with administrators and parents as well as other teachers.

School counselors need to be able to communicate with parents, teachers, and administrators to pass along information on potential problems without fear of reprisal from the administration.

Last, as parents, it is up to us on several levels. We are the closest adults to our kids, so we need to have open lines of communication and know when something is wrong. We need to be appreciative of teachers, counselors, and neighbors who try to advise us of a problem. And we have to demand that the school, teachers, and administrators answer our valid questions.

Without communication, our society shuts down. Without communication with our kids, schools and, more important, families shut down.

Unequal Enforcement of Policies or Perceived Unequal Enforcement

Think back to your high school years. It seemed like the jocks, cheerleaders, and preppies could get away with anything, while the greasers, hards, and misfits got into trouble just for breathing. (I don't know what you called them, but in my school they were greasers or hards if they hung out on the back lawn, talked tough, and smoked cigarettes.) Others were considered misfits if they didn't belong in any group, not even the nerds. All through school, there are cliques; even if you didn't want to be in one, you were, and everyone was identified by the people they hung out with.

We have all seen the end result of unequal treatment of students, so we should balk at blanket sentiments made about any one group. And it should make us fairly upset even if our children aren't involved. It is also called stereotyping, which we will get into later.

Let me first say that we will never know the whole story of how kids are treated if we are not involved. The perception that one child or group of children is getting better treatment than another group can spark an incident of school violence. On the other hand, if a child or groups of children are receiving disparate treatment, there is also a problem.

For example, the star of the football team gets a week of detention because of a graffiti incident, yet a known druggie ends up suspended for a week for the same incident. On the surface, it can be perceived that the jock is getting better treatment, but maybe this is the jock's first time to get in trouble and the other teen's fifteenth time.

In either case, the potential for an incident leading to violence is dependent on the original incident. If the incident involves playing too rough at recess, that's one thing. But cheating, theft, vandalism, arson, etc., can be far worse. And these are only examples of incidents that can spark violence; in some schools, they could start a riot.

Again, I have to point to communication and strict adherence to published policies and procedures. If communication is open and all parties know and understand the rules, then following the policies and procedures is easy. A list of punishments, from first offense to multiple offenses, should be known. It should also be made known that the principal has discretion regarding what punishments are to be meted out. When everyone knows the process, then there are fewer surprises and cries of disparity.

So again, it comes down to communication.

Stereotyping

This is a huge problem in our schools, and it doesn't all come from the kids. Parents, teachers, and police have all stereotyped others. It has happened through the ages.

In the fifties, kids who wore jeans were not to be associated with because they were either poor or couldn't be trusted because they were plain bad news. Girls who laughed too much or too loud or even had a boyfriend too young were termed "loose." In the sixties, people were assumed to be drug-using, free-loving hippies if they wore their hair too long, said "groovy," liked to party, protested the Vietnam War, or were just different. In the seventies … do I need to go on?

Kids are going to stereotype others because they are kids and that is what they have been taught. We as parents, teachers, and administrators need to dissuade our kids from these notions. It is within our power to teach tolerance for everyone.

That said, it isn't going to be easy. Children are very judgmental toward anyone different. Remember thinking differently of a classmate who had a physical disability? Children can be downright cruel. As they grow older, they reinforce those ideas until, when they reach their teen years, they are rock solid in their beliefs.

An incident in Albuquerque, New Mexico, illustrates the point. A teenager, dressed as a punker with a Mohawk and all, liked punk music and hung out with other punkers. He and his friends were social minded and worked for free, painting fences and community centers and cleaning up parks. And yet, because he was different and preferred a lifestyle that was on the "fringe," he was murdered by one of the "good" kids, a football star with rich parents, a cheerleader girlfriend, above-average grades, and a cherry car. He was supposedly someone to look up to because he had it all—except tolerance for anyone different than himself.

Stereotyping works both ways, however. At one time or another, we have all been stereotyped by others. We were the jock or the geek. Maybe we were the short, fat kid who was stupid, like I was. Were you ever called a freakazoid? I used that term myself years ago. And even as the short, fat kid, there were kids that I stereotyped as being either above or below me.

As with the punker in Albuquerque, you never know what is in someone. Another example is Michael Skakel, a handsome young man who was shy around girls. No one ever thought him capable of murder. After all, he was related to the royal family of America, the Kennedy's. Yet one night, he savagely beat Martha Moxley to death. The fact that he was stereotyped as a "good kid" kept him out of prison for nearly three decades.

As parents, do we stereotype kids at school simply based on their appearance? How about the fifteen-year-old who is pregnant? She's obviously a slut, right? Maybe she was raped and doesn't believe in abortion.

Maybe people stereotype you as poor. Why? You ask. Is it because you drive an older car, your clothes aren't brand new, and you work two jobs? They may never consider the fact that you're frugal and saving for your children's college tuition.

Stereotyping is never a good thing. Do you remember the old adage "Never judge a book by its cover"? When did we stop believing in that?

Authoritarian Style Management

The first thing that comes to mind when I think of authoritarian style management is the maxim that I learned when I first started working: "It is my way or the highway." Have you heard that or some derivative of it?

This is essentially an authoritarian style of management. None of us like supervisors or managers who are like that, nor do we necessarily listen to figures who use this style.

In some instances, this style works because it has to, such as in combat zones or other life-or-death situations or even in a school with a serious disciplinary problem.

Joe Clark was the principal of a high school in New York City, and he carried a baseball bat with him whenever he walked the halls. Why? It wasn't for protection. It was to make a point. He broke many lockers, trash cans, and other things, including the bat several times, until he restored discipline and order in the school.

Parents are never handed a manual on how to be a parent. We are handed an eight-pound bundle of poop, drool, and love and told to go parent. That kind of on-the-job training is tenuous at best.

But we grow into the role, and most of us do an adequate job of raising these bundles into responsible adults with little bundles of their own. But they often rebel, and you find yourself asking why. The answer is simple: "You live in my house, and while you're living here, you'll live by my rules!" Sound familiar? Maybe you haven't said those exact words but something close.

And yes, a few pages back I told you to be that way. Let me explain. We can be authoritarian without the Gestapo tactics. (Here comes that word again; see if you can spot it.) If we have communicated effectively with our kids since they were small, then they will know what the limits are and what is and is not acceptable.

Along the same lines, school administrators can do the same thing and still enforce the rules. Some of the best people I've ever known were my principals: Mr. Smith, Mr. Basil Hoehn, and the silver fox Mr. Oltoff. They were all strict disciplinarians, but they were fair and understanding. They took the time to communicate with their students.

We all need someone who is in authority and who acts like that once in a while. But if you're like that constantly, you build resentment, distrust, and a lot of wariness. If you are a strict but caring person, when you get mad, everyone will know instantly you're really pissed off.

Chapter 4

The Warning Signs

This is one major area in which I disagree with many doctors, psychiatrists, and other types of counselors and therapists. They will tell you and the world that too many times, there are no warning signs at all that someone will do something violent. Well, with all due respect for their long periods of learning and knowledge, they are dead wrong. There are always warning signs that a student is about to do something violent. The key is to know the signs and react to them.

Whether we act upon the knowledge that we acquire or decide to ignore it is our choice. There is absolutely no excuse or reason for a parent to say "I didn't know." The only thing that is worse than that is the out-and-out denial. You've seen such parents on TV every time a kid is murdered at school or some other crime is committed. "It can't be my kids. They'd never do anything like that. They're such good kids." We watch the news report, say that the parents are stupid and should have seen it coming, and then deny it when the tables are turned and it is our kid on the news.

Consistently, we as parents make excuses for our children's bad behavior, saying "If only the teacher had seen …" or "If only the bus driver had.…" We see the videos on the TV and Internet of kids beating up on other kids, and no one, not even adults, are stopping it. The aggressors are often clearly shown in the video, and yet the parents make remarks such as, "That's not my kid," "My kid is too good to do that," "My kid was provoked," etc.

This goes back to the parental responsibility chapter. Parents, guardians, and educators need to stop blaming others, take responsibility, and do the right thing. Again, the right thing may not be the most popular or PC thing, but for the sake of the children we need to stand up and do it. As the mentors of the leaders of tomorrow, we need to show our children what personal responsibility is.

When reading about these warning signs, please understand this. One or two of these can be worrisome by themselves, but they are probably indicative of a limited problem in that particular area. It's when you start to see four, five, six, or more that you need to start worrying about the next Columbine. I must restate the point about your child. No one should know your kid better than you. The parents who grow old thinking and worrying about keeping their kids safe from these problems and danger are in the best position to understand the changes happening with their children. And it is in this context that everyone involved with our children needs to be aware of the warning signs and inform others when they observe one. Furthermore, we need to acknowledge and explore the issue, not ignore it thinking it will go away.

The following story is an example of how things can build up and be overlooked and dismissed as ordinary behavior.

Diary of a Plot

This is a simulated diary of a boy who has been pushed too far. I have used incidents from my life in Middle School and High School. The details are fictionalized.

October 10th

Happened again today, Mary talked dirty to me, making me blush, then as usual they all laughed. I was so red I thought my face would burn off.

October 31st

Mr. Q yelled at me again for being lazy and fat. I really tried to climb that rope, but I guess I am just too fat to pull myself up. Then came the showers again. I wish he wouldn't make me shower. I know I'm fat, but my dick is so much smaller than every one else's, I get laughed at there too. Sigh.

November 5th

Sometimes I just wish I was dead and then everyone would care. If I died, then they'd be sorry.

November 20th

Thank God Thanksgiving is coming up. I don't know how much more I can handle. Mr. A asked me what kind of idiot I was in class. I just can't get this electrical stuff. I don't know my ohms from my amps, he says. That bastard said my brain was shorted out. I wish he was dead. Maybe he'll have a car accident during Thanksgiving. One could always hope.

December 8th

So much for car accidents. Both Mr. A and Q told everyone it was okay to laugh at the stupid fat kid because I wouldn't know any better. I hate them so much.

December 18th

Some of the seniors locked me in a locker. I thought I would die. I couldn't breathe. Maybe I should just die. Wish I could take some of them with me. Julie let me out and yelled at them. She is beautiful and a freshman like me. WOW!!!!!!!!

December 20th

Julie and Karen gave me Christmas cards—wow! I think I love both of them. I was floating on cloud 9 until Matt and Allan took them away and tore them up. Then they hit me for crying. I wish they were dead.

January 5th

First day back after Christmas, Julie talked to me today. Hearing her voice is like listening to a robin sing. The day was fine until John and Adam started pushing me around in the locker room after gym. I got snapped with a towel so many times my butt and legs were bleeding, and then they stuck me in the towel bin while everyone else laughed and called me names. I got punched for crying. I wish I could kill them all. Mr. Q told me to shut up and act like a man.

January 10th

The day was horrible. I told Jack that I liked Julie and Karen. Someone must have heard because later they both yelled at me for writing crude and horrible stuff on the bathroom wall about them. They told me I was selfish and called me a whole bunch of really bad names. Then the principal called me in to ask why I had written such filth on the bathroom wall. When I told him I didn't do it, he called me a liar and threatened to suspend me. He gave me detention instead and the worst was yet to come. I saw Jack laughing and pointing at me with a bunch of those other assholes. I thought he was my friend. One of these days.

January 30th

I think I have a solution to my problem. We started studying Hitler today in history. It's interesting how he got rid of those who teased and bullied him when he was younger. I think I have found a new hero, instead of Terry Bradshaw.

February 9th

WOW! Stalin killed millions and people loved him! I wonder if that could work for me. Otherwise it was the same old story today. I hate Mr. A. If I could, I'd blow his brains out. I'd like to see them splattered all over that damned writing board of his. On the bright side Julie apologized for yelling at me. She said that someone told her about the wall, and she just thought I had done it until she heard someone else say they did it and put my name there. After I asked her several times and started to get mad, she told me it was Jack. That back-stabbing bastard will be the first to go.

March 1st

I HAVE HAD ENOUGH!!!!!!!!!!! I'm gonna kill them all!!!!!! Alice laughed at me and got the others to do it too because I was eating my lunch so fast. Well, I wanted to go to the library, but no, they couldn't think of that. The fat kid eats fast so he can get more. Well, I'VE HAD IT!!!!!!!!!!! I found Daddy's gun and I've hidden it in my secret place. I also took a bunch of bullets. I think I can get the other gun later and more bullets. They'll see I'm not a pussy.

March 10th

I got the other gun and tons of bullets. I'll take the propane tanks to the school after dark and hide them. Maybe tomorrow. Soon, very soon, they'll stop teasing me. I'll make them stop Forever!

March 30th

Daddy filed a report with the police about the guns. I also took some of Mommy's jewelry to make it more believable. They'll never think it was me! Ha ha ha ha ha ha ha ha

April 1st

Tomorrow's the day. I'm taking the propane tanks to hide tonight. Hook them together close to the gas main and the whole school will go BOOM! I got the guns hidden in my gym bag and fully loaded. Starting tomorrow they'll all respect me. I'm gonna start with Mr. Q and all those sons of bitches in gym class. I don't think anyone will hear in the locker room. I should get about 9 or 10 of them there.

Then I'm gonna move up to Mr. A's class and take out that bastard. There might be a few others there too. Aw hell, even if I don't know them, they probably deserve to get shot. If not me, they've teased someone else.

They'll respect me after that. I'm going to be the avenging angel taking out those who don't deserve to live just like Hitler and Stalin did. I hope Julie and Karen don't get in the way.

I think after Mr. A's class, I'll wander about and see if I can spot more of those who tease and humiliate me.

I'M TIRED OF BEING TEASED AND HUMILI-ATED!!!!!!! I'LL TEACH THEM A LESSON THEY'LL NEVER FORGET!!!!! EVEN BY GOD THAT BITCH MARY!!!!!!! THEY'LL NEVER DO IT TO ANYONE ELSE OR ME AGAIN!!!!!!

April 2nd

Damn I was a lunatic last night. Wow! But today is the day. I just wanted to write a note good-bye.

Mom and Dad:

I love you and I hope you won't worry about me anymore. By the time you read this, I'll be in a much better place. Do me a favor and tell Julie that I think she is drop-dead pretty and thank her for being the only one to be nice to me at this stinking rotten school.

GOOD-BYE!

Threats

Threats are the most obvious sign that something may be coming down the pipeline. Whether the threat is verbal or on My Space, it needs to be taken seriously. Educators who become aware of threats need to sit the student and parents down and talk with them. Parents need to take appropriate action whether they caught the threat or the school did. The incident can't be swept under the rug. If it is a serious threat, then not only the offending student and his or her parents need to be notified; all the students and parents whose well-being may be in jeopardy need to be notified. If it is an imminent threat, then the police should be contacted. But use a bit of common sense too.

There are four different types of threats heard from students. Understanding the difference can be the key to understanding how dangerous they are.

1. Veiled threats

What constitutes a veiled threat? By pulling a veil across something, you obscure or blur the object behind the veil. Likewise, a veiled threat may not be recognized as a threat.

For example, statements made after losing an athletic contest such as the homecoming football game can sound threatening, such as "I hate those guys. I wish we could kill them next time." These cannot be confused with angry, blurted statements, such as "I hate Steve. I am going to take care of that problem." Generally, angry statements will be backed up by a series of incidents.

Additionally, a veiled threat can be made simply with body language, such as a person tightening his fists when speaking about a certain individual, smacking his fist into the palm of the other hand, white-knuckling the steering wheel or pounding it when discussing the person, clenching jaws or teeth, or twisting objects like pens, pencils, and pieces of wood or metal. Generally, veiled threats are the most difficult to recognized as threats because they are most often made either alone or in the presence of only one or two other people. Almost as often, the mutterings and ramblings under one's breath will not be recognized as threatening, this leads us to our next point.

2. **Open and verbal threats**

These are threats that are vocalized or written for everyone to see or hear. Often, these are very loud and accompanied by a sharp argument or other violent behavior between the individuals involved.

As with the cry at the losing homecoming game, these threats are angry, vehement, and nasty, with all the body language mentioned in the last section. The persons making these threats have anger control issues and don't care who overhears what they are saying. They want the whole world to know what they are planning and don't care about the consequences.

3. **Private, verbal/written threats**

This type of threat is usually issued in a cool, calm, collected manner. Threats of this type are characterized not by the angry, loud nature of those discussed above but are often written on individuals' My Space, Facebook, or other personal Web sites. They are often spoken to many different people as well. The threat is considered private simply because of the way the threat is passed along—person to person. Kids know that what is placed on the Internet can remain there for a long time and that anyone can access it, and they know that speaking to a few of their friends will ensure that the threat makes the rounds so that everyone will know of it. These types of students are usually more dangerous than others because they have such tight control over their emotions.

4. **Written threats and vandalism**

These types of threats are both the least serious and the most serious. Okay, now you really think I'm off my rocker. How can they be both serious and not?

The type of written threats being discussed here are those written in journals, diaries, notebooks, and other forms of free expression, which we will discuss in detail later. Graffiti threats—that is, vandalism—are rarely, if ever, serious, credible threats. While both of these threats need to be investigated, the overall picture of the student involved needs to be assessed before action is taken.

Attendance Problems

If a student has recently started to have problems getting to school on time or attending at all, then you may have the beginnings of a problem that may or may not be serious. If the child has always had this type of problem, then it may not be a symptom of a larger issue. On the flip side, if the student has always had exemplary attendance and then suddenly begins to show tardiness, even between classes, or stops showing up for class altogether, it needs to be looked at with the expectation of resolving the issue.

Attendance and tardiness issues have many potential causes. The child may be experiencing health concerns or problems that cause fatigue and listlessness. She may have a parent going through a job change or working hours that conflict with being able to get the child ready for school in the same timely manner as before. Or the parents may require the child to be more involved at home with younger siblings, and therefore the child is getting less rest than before.

Attendance problems could also be the result of bullying. If a child does not want to confront a bully, she may take a longer route to school or just wait until school starts, when she knows the bully is already in class and she'll be safe. She may linger in a class until break time is almost over to be sure the bully is not in the hallways when moving between classes.

Schoolwork Issues

Ah, good old schoolwork. Now, where did I put mine? Oh, that's right, the cat ate it. No wait, my dad was, uh … had to go on a secret mission. Yeah, that's it! What'd you say? Oh well, it didn't work in math class either.

Most of us never had a problem keeping up with or completing homework or class work on time. We've occasionally lapses where we didn't do our assignments or couldn't get it all done on time, but for the most part we could keep up.

And we've all been a little sick at times, causing our work to suffer in quality. Or we've been just plain lazy in doing a good job on that book report on *War and Peace.*

But for the teenager who may be having problems and thinking about doing violence, it goes a lot deeper than that.

Their work patterns are inconsistent at best, and their study habits are even worse. One week, they may be working like a hound dog during a fox hunt, and the next they're playing a bloodhound on a lazy spring day.

For an example, let's look at Steve, an average sixteen-year-old sophomore who normally has a C average. But for one week, he is manic about his work in all his classes, almost obsessive. He gets A's for the entire week. The next week he's down to D's, then B's and C's, and then back to A's. The pattern is that he's high one week or day and down the next on the same material.

Is he cheating? Maybe someone else is doing his homework. There is an answer to this, and it's none of the above. Steve is simply having problems with something or someone. What is bothering him we don't know, but we can see the results in his work.

Steve's mother has noticed lately that Steve seems to work intensively some nights, rarely coming out of his room to eat or use the bathroom. There are some weeks when she wonders if he's using drugs because he works so intently. But other weeks, he doesn't do much of anything. Is she right about the drugs?

She could be. But it could be just as likely that he's having other social issues, is depressed, or is getting sick. In any event, Steve's mom and his teachers are seeing the same thing, just from different angles.

Is all this indicative of a larger problem? It could be. Or Steve could be just a normal teenager trying to adjust to the ever-changing world we live in, not to mention dealing with all those outrageous, over-the-top, raging, surging, and irrepressible testosterone levels. You know the ones that take boys and turn them into drooling, googoly-eyed rejects when a pretty girl walks by.

The only way to know is for Steve's mom to communicate with him. We as parents should know our kids better than anyone outside of their friends. We should know if there is a problem, and the only way to know that is to communicate. Yeah, I know I'm pounding that rock into dust. But are you a parent that your teenager can trust because you've built that?

Consistent Bullying and Teasing

Children who are consistently bullied or teased are at risk of turning the tables on their tormentors and silencing the bullies forever. Children who feel trapped by bullies may feel they have no alternative but to fight back, even to the extreme, which could mean bringing a firearm or knife to school for protection or aggression.

I was severely bullied and teased from eighth grade to my junior year in high school. I was short, fat, shy, and naive. I was so inept at my shop and physical ed classes that even the teachers embarrassed and humiliated me. Yet I never made a hit list or threatened anyone. There were two reasons I didn't: 1) I'm the poster boy for Murphy's Law—anything that could go wrong would go wrong If I tried anything, and 2) I didn't know how to kill anything bigger than a bug back then. Besides, I didn't want to get into trouble.

Megan Cayton, a Maricopa County, Arizona, teen probation officer, offers the following:

Bullying occurs at all ages in any walk of life. From what I recall personally and from conversations that have occurred over the years, throughout adolescence and elementary school, kids are pretty cruel. I believe not only do the parents need to boost their child's self-esteem if they are the victim; they also need to hold a consequence and discipline their children if they are the actual bully. The same tactics need to be followed through within the school systems. In addition, it needs to be followed through to outside extracurricular activities. I believe that all citizens should be held accountable to help enforce that such actions will not be tolerated. Unfortunately, lack of communication is a huge issue; along with lack of knowledge with regard to the effects that bullying have on an individual. Anyone can "snap" at any time in life. Hopefully, along the way, persons have utilized coping skills and tools that they have hopefully learned from infant to toddler through adolescence to adulthood. I truly believe that there should be courses/classes on bullying.

As I have discovered in my years of researching workplace violence, if a person is bullied and teased into a corner, he is likely to come out swinging. The majority of our kids don't have the skills necessary to handle that kind of stress, and neither do many adults.

An interesting twist in the bullying issue is the potential for flipping the situation. What I mean is that, eventually, the victim will fight back against the tormentor, who will then escalate the abuse, sometimes taking it to the extreme. In other words, the bully doesn't want to lose face to the victim, so the bully increases the abuse to make the victim toe the line. An example is a teen who suffered from alopecia (hair loss). He developed a tough-guy persona to deal with all the teasing. When one boy teased him too much, the teen confronted him on the school bus. The bully felt he had lost face in front of the other kids, and two days later he brought a gun to school and killed the boy in the cafeteria.

Tips for Parents

If your child might be affected by an incident of bullying or hazing, here are some things you should do according to Florida Atlantic University Professor of School Counseling Education Elizabeth Villares:

- Talk about the incident with your child.
- Make sure your child knows his or her rights and what to do in the future if another incident occurs.

- Monitor your child's My Space and Facebook sites online to make sure students are not discussing the incident in an inappropriate manner.
- Monitor your child's progress in school closely to make sure he or she has not become distracted in class, which could be a sign of repressed emotions related to the incident.

Also, the American School Counseling Association has a bully-prevention packet on its Web site, www. schoolcounselor.org. This is a good resource to help you understand bullying.

Depression

This is one of the biggest indicators of all and one that I can't talk about intelligently other than to show you what the warning signs of depression are. The kids who perpetrate school crimes are depressed. They feel powerless to control their world, which can, in turn, lead to related problems such as bullying or becoming the stereotypical loner, associating only with other "misfits." Additionally, kids who are depressed can seek revenge and can be considered suicidal. They have the need to control some part of their world, no matter how small, and this can manifest itself in several ways and for several reasons, such as family problems (divorce, drug-addicted or alcoholic parents, etc.).

The only thing I can tell you about depression is that unless you know the person, you may not recognize the depression. A person who is depressed may show no outward signs to most people. She will appear happy, congenial, and even sociable. But on the inside, she is falling into her own socks. Like a good actor, she shows happiness even though she is miserable on the inside.

The following is a list of signs and symptoms of depression, taken from Healthline.com.

Childhood social withdrawal
Crying
Difficulty sleeping
Excessive sleep
Fear
Feeling empty
Feeling hopeless
Feeling of anger
Feeling of suicidal intent
Flat affect
Guilt
Headache
Increased appetite
Irritability
Lethargy
Loss of appetite
Loss of capacity for enjoyment
Loss in interest in previously enjoyable activities
Memory impairment
Monotone voice
Mood swings
Neglected appearance
Nervousness
Night sweats
Outbursts of anger
Planning suicide
Poor hygiene
Poor self-esteem
Problem behavior
Problems at work/school
Self-depreciation
Social isolation
Social withdrawal
Sudden awakening
Suicidal thoughts
Thoughts about dying
Thoughts about suicide
Intentional weight loss
Weight gain
Weight loss
withdrawn behavior

Continual Excuses

This is just as much a social issue as it is a warning sign and parental issue. Of course, teens have been making excuses to get out of trouble and to avoid talking to parents for millennia. But this is an ever-growing social problem as well.

In today's society, few people take responsibility for what they do, and to the detriment of our kids and society, it's rubbing off. Our kids are by no means stupid and are fairly good observers.

They see on the news that a politician knowingly lies to the cameras and denies responsibility for some wrongdoing. They then turn around and see us, their parents, do the same thing at work or out in public. Even in school, they see it occur with teachers and the staff.

And when we tell them that they must be responsible for what they do, they figure, why should they? Everywhere they look, no one owns up to their messes.

As I stated above, teenagers are good at avoiding responsibility for most things simply because they are teenagers. But when the simplest of mistakes elicits an excuse, then there might be a problem.

As a society, we also encourage victim hood. In other words, we often claim that our problems are someone else's fault because they did something to cause us to do what we did. "The teacher doesn't like me. That's why I got an F." "I'm disabled and someone else must take care of me because they owe it to me." "I failed my book report because you didn't make me read that book, Mom."

While I've spent time blasting a society of excuse makers, the point is that teenagers make excuses for a lot of things. When they begin making excuses for minor, trivial things they haven't make excuses for in the past you should be wondering what's wrong. What's changed? It's just that damned group of friends they hang around with, right?

Time Impact

Everybody needs time with their kids, spouses, supervisors, and others every day. Teenagers are no different. They need time with their friends and parents, and they need time with their teachers.

I understand how hard it is to get one-on-one time with a teacher in today's classrooms. With only fifty minutes or so in a class period and usually more than twenty-five students per class, the time is fleeting. Devoting time to each student can seem like an impossible task.

But somehow teachers make time for most students and their questions. We've already discussed the deficiencies in teachers' knowing their students, so we won't discuss that here. But with roughly one and a half minutes for each student per class, there is just not a lot of time for personal, face-to-face talks or help. And that's where the impact on time enters the equation in school violence, whether it is assaults, bullying, or murder.

It usually starts out small. A student will need an extra few seconds on an assignment this week, and then next week he'll need a few more seconds. Before they are aware of it, within a few weeks, teachers may be spending as much as ten minutes with one student. And that doesn't help the other students.

The teacher may refer the student to a counselor for help in selecting less challenging classes or to find out why he's not getting the material. In many cases, that's all that's needed.

But let's take a student who begins to become disruptive. It started with extra time needed to learn the material, which can be disruptive enough. Then the student begins acting up, which requires a few minutes for the teacher to send him to the office. Then it takes another five minutes to quell the unrest of the others. That's as much as fifteen minutes lost.

In the principal's office (or vice principal's), it takes fifteen to thirty minutes to discuss the problem with the student and possibly refer him to the counselor for another thirty-minute discussion.

In the counselor's office, the student spends another thirty to sixty minutes discussing the issue, and that time may just lead to more sessions. Then, of course, there is always detention.

Detention takes a teacher or other administrators away from other work and projects. Who knows what the cost of one hour per day of detention can be?

After several weeks of needing just a little more time each day, teachers and administrators are expending more than three hours for a single incident. That may not seem like a lot, but with the myriad of other students and projects that need to be completed, it is an enormous expenditure of time.

And what about calling the parents? They may have to take several hours away from work to attend a meeting in the principal's office. So then the parents get even more harried than before, adding more stress.

By the time a student has become a bona fide threat to commit a Columbine style of attack; he has taken more than forty hours of effort from the school, staff, and resources! That's an entire workweek of time devoted to one troubled teenager. If that time is devoted to helping the student uncover the root cause of the problem, that's okay. But spending the time on that student instead of other students cannot be tolerated.

Time is crucial for everyone. Teachers have to manage their time better than most and help the most students, but they have to balance that with the time needed to spot the warning signs, discuss these problems with others, assist in solving their problems, and still teaching their other students, not to mention taking any personal time they may wish to have.

While it may be the easy way out to simply send students to the office for others to deal with, teachers are the ones who have to spot the increased amount of time being spent on one student. Again, that amount of time can creep up on them, but they need to know their students, manage their time, and notify someone if a student demands an inordinate amount of it.

Does a student having a few problems with geometry indicate that he's going to shoot up the school? No. Like every thing else in the chapter, we have to look at the larger picture and overall behaviors as well.

Entertainment

You were probably wondering when I would get around to discussing this one, and I'm sure you're expecting a condemnation of all video games and music. Actually, I'm not going to condemn all of it, only most of it.

As we discussed in the section on parental responsibility, we decide what entertainment our kids can enjoy. It's us who allow those violent games into the house for them to play.

But it has been observed in many cases that the perpetrators of school violence have immersed themselves in entertainment that is not appropriate for them. And how do we know that it affects our kids in a demoralizing way (for us at least)?

In December 2008, a six-year-old and a seven-year-old boy were taken into custody by the Maricopa County Sheriff's Department in Arizona. Why? After playing the game Grand Theft Auto for several hours, they found a four-month-old kitten and killed it. They stoned it to death and then hung it by its neck from a tree in a neighbor's yard with a game controller cord. They had to stand on tiptoe to reach the branch they hung it from.

These boys were never charged because in Arizona they are too young to be charged with any crime. However, they have a head start on taking a knife or handgun to school to solve a problem. They've already killed once and thought nothing about it.

With the violent video games; rap music that glorifies killing, rape, degradation of women, drug dealing, and using drugs; movies that are nothing but violent blood splatter everywhere; and television that shows murder, mayhem, and destructive behavior on a regular basis, is it any wonder that our kids are desensitized to these things?

And yes, that's what it is—desensitization. Many studies have reported that the number of murders a child views before turning twelve is somewhere in the thousands.

Children have intelligence, but they are also very impressionable. If you tell children from a young age that all women are whores and are good for only one thing, then they will grow up believing that. And of course your choice of entertainment for them has a profound impact on them.

There is a large difference in the violence that the baby boomer and early Generation X'ers experienced and what the Generation Y'ers and the millennium babies have witnessed. We grew up knowing we couldn't drop an anvil on Billy's head.

We had our violent television programs—*Gunsmoke, Star Trek, Starsky and Hutch*. We had our music with sex and violence in more forms than I can count. But we knew what was out of bounds. Our parents taught us what the difference between fantasy and reality was.

Unfortunately, today we don't teach right from wrong or fantasy from reality. Our children are being taught that there are no limits and that they can do whatever makes them feel good about themselves and not feel guilty about it. They hear it at home, at school, in movie theatres, in their cars, and virtually everywhere else.

As parents, teachers, and concerned members of society, we need to teach our children that not everything that makes them feel good about themselves is good for them or anyone else. Just because marijuana makes you feel good doesn't mean it's good for your body.

Sex is one of the most pleasurable acts in the world. And because we have not taught kids to abstain or at least take care, we have a proliferation of teen pregnancies and STDs.

Murdering a classmate, parent, or someone else you hate may make you feel better for a little while, but eventually your conscience, and justice, catches up with you. And the consequences are not usually very attractive.

As long as we allow the impressionable minds of children and teenagers to be influenced by sex, violence, and drugs, we will have the threat that the kid next door will kill you because you "disrespected" him by looking at him wrong or told him to behave.

Free Expression

With all respect and deference to the First Amendment right to free speech, sometimes those words can be a cry for threats. We discussed threats earlier, but we're getting into territory here that goes beyond words.

Children, especially boys, are usually enamored of weapons of any kind. From a sword in a book on King Arthur to the carbine that Sergeant York used to capture twenty-three Germans during World War I, boys like weapons and like to draw them.

Free expression crosses the line from a First Amendment right to a warning sign of violence when the imagery is combined with other items.

There are numerous cases of a child—usually a boy—being suspended, expelled, or worse simply because he drew a doodle of a firearm. In some cases, the assignment was to draw something that made him happy, and he happened to be a hunter!

What kind of words are they using? Are they writing "kill," "death," "torture" and so on in class work or private journals? And does it matter? The answer to that is unequivocally no. If it is within the framework of class work, then why condemn them?

Now, if the assignment is innocuous, such as writing about the happiest Christmas, and a student turns in a paper on how he used his new .22 caliber Mossberg to shoot and kill little furry animals for no other reason than to try it out, then that could be cause for alarm. But again, it could just be youthful exuberance and the result of no responsibility taught in the home.

Does the fact that a teenager is drawing pictures of rifles, death, killing, handguns, and the like mean he is about to do something violent? Absolutely not. It may be cause for concern, but the right first step is to communicate with the child and parents first.

At Virginia Tech in 2007, Cho Seung-Hui wrote some very dark passages in his English class that frightened his English instructor to the point that she notified the administration and had him removed from her class. She described them as dark, homicidal, and frightening. He often used rich white kids as his targets in his writings, but Cho exhibited other warning signs as well. Then there was Dylan Klebold and Eric Harris, who put together an advertisement for a class project. The assignment was to form a business and then film or record a commercial for their business. The name they chose for their business was Hitmen for Hire, a telling clue of what was to come— it was turned in just one week before the shootings. The commercial showed a student who wanted another student killed, and the end result was a satisfied customer.

Think about Stephen King and Dean Koontz. If they were writing for a class now, they would both be expelled. Their writings are dark, menacing, and just plain scary. But, at least outwardly, they show no signs of going postal.

Free expression falls into that realm that I call the zero-tolerance zone, a place where common sense doesn't exist and there are no gray areas. It allows the punishment of girls for sharing a Midol for PMS or accidentally bringing a plastic knife to school and voluntarily turning it in. In most instances, a child would be suspended for those infractions.

The key is to use common sense when reading or viewing students' doodles or writings. Whether it is for a class assignment or in a personal journal, ask yourself if the student has exhibited any other warning signs and whether he or she is a likely one to commit some act of violence.

The First Amendment protects our right to say or draw anything we want but does not give us the right to terrorize or frighten. Many school districts have egg on their faces because their actions in response to drawings or writings become public knowledge. Do writings and doodles offer signs? Absolutely, but look at the whole picture, not just the notebook.

Poor Relationship Skills

People with poor relationship skills are usually described as geeks, loners, weirdo's, or mental, and in many respects the descriptions could be right. These groups of people seem to be on the outs with practically everyone, sometimes even themselves.

But even those who are gregarious can have poor skills in forming relationships, much less maintaining them. And while they may seem comfortable around lots of friends, what they're probably feeling inside is isolation.

Let's liken this to the most gorgeous girl in school who at the time doesn't have a boyfriend. She probably doesn't have a date Friday night because everyone assumes that she does have a date!

There may be a medical reason for some people's poor relationship skills. Some teenagers who have ADHD also have a condition known as Asperser's syndrome, which makes them so awkward socially that while they want to be sociable, few will associate with them.

I have a close friend whose daughter has both ADHD and Asperser's. The daughter is loud, abrasive, and socially inept. She so desperately wants friends and to be liked that she cries sometimes because she's not.

There are other reasons for poor relationships. A child's family may move a lot and she is always the new kid, and you know how that can be. A child may be just painfully shy or have low self-esteem. While I'm not a proponent of this philosophy, I believe it's important for kids to have good self-esteem.

Another reason for poor relationship skills can be physical or sexual abuse at home, or even at school, although that is very rare. Children who have been abused usually have a tendency to be loners. And then there is also emotional abuse. One of the best warning signs for emotional abuse is low self-esteem.

Again, I'm not an expert in this area, and I don't feel comfortable discussing it other than in the context above. But I can give you the warning signs of physical and sexual abuse.

The following signs may signal the presence of child abuse or neglect.

The child exhibits these attributes:

- Shows sudden changes in behavior or school performance
- Has not received help for physical or medical problems brought to the parents' attention
- Has learning problems (or difficulty concentrating) that cannot be attributed to specific physical or psychological causes
- Is always watchful, as though preparing for something bad to happen
- Lacks adult supervision
- Is overly compliant, passive, or withdrawn
- Comes to school or other activities early, stays late, and does not want to go home

The parent exhibits these attributes:

- Shows little concern for the child
- Denies the existence of, or blames the child for, the child's problems in school or at home
- Asks teachers or other caretakers to use harsh physical discipline if the child misbehaves
- Sees the child as entirely bad, worthless, or burdensome
- Demands a level of physical or academic performance the child cannot achieve

- Looks primarily to the child for care, attention, and satisfaction of emotional needs

The parent and child, together, exhibit these behaviors:

- Rarely touch or look at each other
- Consider their relationship to be entirely negative
- State that they do not like each other
- This information was adapted from *Recognizing Child Abuse: What Parents Should Know*. Prevent Child Abuse America. ©2003.

Signs of Sexual Abuse

The presence of a single sign does not prove child abuse is occurring in a family; however, when these signs appear repeatedly or in combination, you should take a closer look at the situation and consider the possibility of child abuse.

Consider the possibility of sexual abuse when the **child** does the following:

- Has difficulty walking or sitting
- Suddenly refuses to change for gym or to participate in physical activities
- Reports nightmares or bedwetting
- Experiences a sudden change in appetite
- Demonstrates bizarre, sophisticated, or unusual sexual knowledge or behavior
- Becomes pregnant or contracts a venereal disease, particularly if under the age of fourteen

- Runs away
- Reports sexual abuse by a parent or another adult caregiver
- Consider the possibility of sexual abuse when the **parent or other adult caregiver** does the following:
- Is unduly protective of the child or severely limits the child's contact with other children, especially of the opposite sex
- Is secretive and isolated
- Is jealous or controlling with family members
- This information was adapted from *Recognizing Child Abuse: What Parents Should Know*. Prevent Child Abuse America. ©2003.

What Should You Look for If You Suspect Sexual Abuse?

Symptoms of sexual abuse in older children and adolescents include the following:

- Depression
- Nightmares or sleep disturbances
- Poor school performance
- Promiscuity
- Substance abuse
- Aggression
- Running away from home
- Fear of attack recurring
- Eating disturbances

- Early pregnancy or marriage
- Suicidal gestures
- Anger about being forced into situation beyond one's control
- Pseudo-mature behaviors

Alcohol/Drug Abuse

What are the signs of alcohol or drug abuse? Some of the most noticeable signs would be things such as smelling alcohol on your child's breath, assuming your child is not diabetic. Remember, if a person's blood sugar is really out of whack, his breath can smell like he's been drinking Boone's Farm Strawberry Hill. Is the liquor in your cabinet disappearing, or does it taste watered down? A quick ploy for teens is to steal liquor from their parents, either by the drink or by the bottle. If you take a drink of your Glenfiddich and it tastes watered down, chances are someone's been nipping and replacing it with water.

Your teen may have a drinking problem if she comes home with a glazed, distant, or happy look in her eyes and smelling of liquor. Additionally, she'll be stumbling around and unsteady on her feet. She may also be overly aggressive, maudlin, or very happy. Always ensure that it's not a medical emergency before addressing the situation as a drinking problem.

And since time began, the best way to know is to actually catch teens drinking, whether from your cabinet or with the liquor in their possession. This goes for drugs as well. Your medicine cabinet is a good place to look, as are their backpacks.

Torturing or Killing Small Animals

You may wonder how many kids really torture or kill animals. The honest answer is that nearly all children will tease the neighborhood stray dog or cat at some point. For the animal, it's probably torment and torture. "Oh come on! How is teasing the same as torture?"

That point is simple. How would you or your child feel if people ten or twenty times your size started throwing rocks, sticks, or other stuff at you? How about being poked with sticks or tied up by the leg or neck? Would you call that torture? Probably so. I would myself.

As parents, when our little darlings come home with a bite or scratch from that stray, what's the first thing we want to do? We want to go and kill it or call animal control to destroy it, even though we, indirectly, provoked its response. The teenager may have been teased too often as well.

Am I one of the crowd that believes all actions against animals are torture and killing? No. I believe that most animals are on this earth to provide humans with something we need, such as food, clothing, and companionship. But I do not believe in torturing or killing animals for the fun of it.

As an example, I don't hunt. My reasoning is simple: I don't like the taste of wild meat. Do I protest deer hunting or other sport as such? No. As long as the animal is used for food, hides, etc., I don't object. I do object to the slaughter for the pure sport of killing, however, as when hunters leave the carcass behind to rot.

A society that allows its youngest to torture, maim, and kill simply because the animal is a nuisance or is smaller than they are will find that human life will also soon to be a nuisance.

Poor Health and Hygiene

At first glance, you might think that poor health and hygiene is not applicable as a warning sign. But if you will follow the logic below, you'll see how it relates to school violence.

The 1990s ushered in the age of grunge. Teenagers all over the country followed in the footsteps of such cultural icons as Pearl Jam and Hole with their long, greasy hair and their torn, dirty, and faded jeans.

There was even a song parody by "Weird Al" Yankovic, "Smells Like Nirvana," that captured this new obsession with being dirty and grungy. How this started and why, I'm still at a loss to explain, and I lived through it! But suffice it to say that, for the most part, grunge has gone the way of the Edsel.

And while it may be just a sign of teenage rebellion, lack of personal hygiene is often a sign of a troubled youth. By not caring about their hygiene, teens may have given up on the world and may be silently shouting, "Why bother?"

Depression, loneliness, stress, and other problems may leave them too harried to notice their lack of hygiene. And most people will not confront others to tell them they stink. They will ignore and stay away from them, further isolating the teens from society and school, making them feel alone and more prone to lash out.

Keep in mind that there may be other issues at work as well. Financial hardship may leave a family unable to purchase hygiene supplies, or they may be literally homeless, with no place to wash themselves, much less their clothes.

On the other hand, poor health may also lead a teenager to believe it's better to go out in a blaze of glory. Pain, social ostracism, depression, and other factors can lead some kids to thinking like that.

Conditions such as liver problems and intestinal disorders can cause serious issues with both health and body odor. Chronic health problems are more likely to fall into this category. Such issues can literally wear someone down. Even multiple sclerosis can cause hygiene problems.

Teasing and bullying of kids with chronic illnesses just forces them into a corner, and, eventually, the cornered will come out swinging, much like a trapped rat. Remember, kids can be cruel toward other children.

Frustration at not being accepted for whatever the reason can push teens over the edge, and if they feel like their lives are not worth anything because of health reasons, they may decide to take a few tormentors with them.

Safety Issues

Let's face it, most teenagers are clumsy. Unless they're athletes, they will walk into walls, trip over invisible ropes, and be unable to hold their books and walk at the same time. Hell, some of us have those problems as adults.

But when the clumsiness becomes overwhelming, it can be a problem, and it can mean several things. It could be related to stress over finals or that new, pretty redhead down the block—remember Charlie Brown?

Or it could mean something much more sinister and dark. Teens may be clumsy because they are preoccupied by the social issues at school—the bullying and teasing they face. They may not discuss this treatment with anyone, not parents, teachers, co-workers, or even best friends.

On the other hand, safety and concentration issues could be related to a medical problem. ADHD is a common diagnosis. Getting diagnosed and receiving treatment can end the problem.

While I believe that a doctor should diagnose a child for ADHD or other problems, I don't think parents should take the first diagnosis. Many times, children are said to have ADHD but actually have a simple food allergy that makes them clumsy and unable to concentrate.

Before beginning any regimen of drugs, get a second opinion. Also try taking the child to a homeopathic (naturopathic) doctor as well. Americans tend to over drug our kids simply to control them better, and recent studies have shown that it can be detrimental to their health. Okay, enough of that soapbox.

As I stated before, teenagers are clumsy anyway, but if their clumsiness begins to result in more than skinned knees and sore shoulders, you have to pay attention. If a teenager is normally not that clumsy and then starts taking trips up the stairs, bumping into doors more often, or walking into trash cans, you need to begin asking why.

The same goes for driving the car. Let's say that your teen is a safe driver who always uses seatbelts, uses turn signals, and looks before starting out, and so on. Then he starts backing over the trash cans regularly or begins collecting speeding tickets. Maybe he just hits the curb when parallel parking although he never used to.

Here's that word again: *communicate* with them and try to get to the bottom of what is bothering them—schoolwork, finals, headaches, teasing, etc. They will roll their eyes and say, "Oh Dad! Geez, nothing's wrong." But you have to keep talking to find out.

New Religious Fervor

As a society, we are becoming more intolerant of religions of all types. Many people are rabidly anti-Semitic and anti-Catholic, and just as many do not like Muslims. Still others abhor anything Christian, and others have an overwhelming dislike for anything other than their own religious preferences, be they Islamic or Christian.

As we discussed earlier, a young mind is prone to being brainwashed. Feed people enough information about one belief, and they have a tendency to believe it. And most teenagers have a desire to believe in something.

But the way this works is that a teenager becomes so enamored by the religion of her choice that she is willing to kill those who are nonbelievers. And before you say anything, it works both ways.

In the Middle East, some Muslims are bent on the destruction of Western civilization and Eastern religions. In many areas, there are Christians who are hell bent on destroying Jews. In yet other countries, Hindus are pitted against Muslims and Sikhs. And finally, let us not forget about Northern Ireland, where they tried to destroy one another in the name of religion for decades.

So while this may not have been specifically scientifically proven, it is worth mentioning. As we crawl further into the twenty-first century, this will certainly be a fuse on a powder keg, and the world interferes with our kids eventually.

Obsession with the Military or the Police

All little boys at one time or another play army with the other kids in the neighborhood, and some of them actually dream of a career in the military. They dream of being the general, leading their soldiers into battle—all quite invigorating and chest-thumping good stuff.

Likewise, most of the boys I grew up with, have raised, or have been around like to play cops and robbers.

Along with many other childhood dreams, they want to be policemen so they can ride around in those cool cars, catch criminals, and make their city safe.

I believe that those are honorable and worthy careers for both boys and girls. In this great country of ours, there is nothing better than serving the country and its citizenry, especially in keeping it safe from its enemies, whether they be foreign terrorists or politicians.

But there comes a point at which an obsession with the military and police might be considered detrimental to a teenager's growth, both physically and mentally. Who knows what that point is? Unless you know your child well, no one will know.

A few things should alert you to this obsession becoming dangerous—maybe. Maybe? Yes, maybe, because it all depends on your child and whether he has any other problems or warning signs.

If a teenager who is dark, brooding, and not into hunting starts wearing camouflage clothes, then you should pay attention. Has he been watching lots of police or military shows?

If you have cable or satellite television, just go through the channels to see the proliferation of cop shows. Some of them are fairly graphic and show us the worst of the human element, and they are on every hour of the day and night.

They are shown on the Arts and Entertainment Network, the Military History Channel, Court TV, and the entire alphabet of broadcast networks as well. We are overwhelmed by police and military shows. And while learning what officers and soldiers do and how they do it is important—learning about the Bataan Death March is always good—consider whether your teen is studying them for ideas.

Police tactics and military strategy are two things that teenagers would be interested in if they were planning a Columbine-style attack. They would want to know how the police operate and how to stealthily attack a target.

In addition to those types of shows, there are police dramas of a different sort. On the cable channels, there is always a good documentary on serial killers. Does your teenager show a high level of interest in such programs? If he does, does that mean …? Not necessarily. Again, he might just be interested in crime and police work, and the same goes for shows about torture through the ages.

Aside from watching television for hours and seeing a continuous stream of violence, even on broadcast networks, does your teenager read crime stories about serial killers as well as books on military strategy? Once more, it may be just an interest in police work or the result of every little boy's dream of being a general.

Practically every little boy and even some girls, like my wife, are enamored with law enforcement and a military career at one point in their lives. Some of them play army, have toy guns, wear fatigues, and decorate their rooms in a military fashion.

But let's remember: at one time, cop shows were some of the highest-rated television shows there were, not to mention military ones. Are we forgetting *Combat* and *Rat Patrol*? What about *Starsky and Hutch*, *Hawaii Five-O*, and *Law and Order*, which has been running for more than fifteen years? We all enjoyed these shows, and some of us devoured them ravenously. But we never plotted the overthrow of the jocks, preps, or nerds.

As with every other warning sign, except threats, you have to look for a pattern. Is this a passing fascination or something more sinister? Do they really want to be a policeman or soldier and are they just gathering information? Only you can tell.

Unusual or Changed Behavior

This is a loaded sign. In order to know if your child has changed, you need to know your child. That makes this mainly a parent issue.

By changed behavior, I am referring to things like wild mood swings, feeling depressed, not enjoying the things they used to, etc. Teenagers are usually full of contradictions as a natural course of events, but this goes beyond the normal rushing of hormones.

Unusual behavior is something else. Have they started picking flowers out of thin air, or maybe dust mites? Are they scrubbing their bathroom with a toothbrush or talking in metaphysical terms? These may be extremes, but

I'm sure you get the idea. Your child may not exhibit such extreme behavior changes.

Do they have a newly acquired interest in police or military tactics? They may also take an interest in mass murderers, especially those who have committed school shootings.

It doesn't really matter what is causing the new behavior; it's whether or not it is indicative of a larger problem that is at issue. Parents need to know their children well enough to know if their children's behavior has changed. Again, *communication* is the key to knowing your child's behavior.

Chapter 5

Security Measures to Discuss with Your School

Now it's time to pay the piper. You've read through all of the sections about warning signs, parental responsibility, and school accountability. Now it's time for what you may think is the most boring part of this book: security.

Security is an integral part of keeping our children safe in our schools, just as it is where you work. I've heard all the slams against having security that there is, and I counter them succinctly.

"Security is just management's way of keeping an eye on us." "It's just a waste of time." "It's just another way to hassle us and keep us from working." "Why do I need a badge? I've worked here for years."

There are plenty more of those statements. But the truth is that a good security program is designed to keep you safe and ensure that the business isn't exposed to crime, especially crime that may cause it to close permanently, depending on the incident.

The same goes for our children. Security is needed at schools just as much as it is needed at a business. When you start to think it's just too intrusive, consider this: would you want anyone to be able to walk in and take out school equipment or wander the halls freely? Of course, these things do happen.

So security at our schools is vital to the education and well-being of our children. Most schools, however, have little or no security, and that is a very scary thought, not only from a safety perspective but from a monetary standpoint as well.

When theft and vandalism occur in any form, it hurts our kids. Due to theft and vandalism, money has to be diverted from other areas to either clean up or replace items that have been stolen or damaged. All that does is increase our taxes and force cutbacks on other programs such as athletics, music, and art.

Most schools and school districts have security measures in place, but they won't necessarily tell you about them for several reasons. One of those reasons is the desire to keep a potential shooter from knowing exactly what is going to happen on campus if an incident occurs, which is a legitimate reason. If you have ever played poker, you know to keep your hole card secret.

But there are other reasons as well. Some schools don't have a security plan simply because they have no time or money to create one. Other schools do have one, but it was written just after World War II and no one knows where to find it. Still others are secretive about their plans because they don't want parents knowing how vulnerable they truly are.

As a parent, it is your right and responsibility to know what security is provided for your children. Should the school lay out its security protocols and plan in a manual for all to see? Of course not, but as parents, we do need to know the basics.

Therefore, you should demand to know these things from your school. Ask the principal at the school, write letters to the district, and attend board meetings. And don't just ask for security procedures; make recommendations too! Don't just complain. Do something to help.

As for security possibly being too restrictive in our schools, trust me, it's not. The ideas that I'm giving you in this chapter are basic. They are the most basic tenets in any physical security program and will cost little if any money to implement.

In the beginning of this book, I stated that we can never fully guarantee our children's safety at school, no matter how restrictive the security measures are. I can design a system of security for any business or school that would make the federal prison officials in Leavenworth, Kansas, proud. But none of us want that.

Not only would it resemble a Soviet-era gulag, but it would be so expensive that our taxes would at least quadruple from what they are now. And, again, no one wants that level of security at our schools, which are supposed to encourage openness, freedom, and the exchange of ideas, not thoughts of escaping on the laundry truck.

Access Control

The most basic element in any security program is access control. Without knowing who you are going to let into your business or school, you have no idea of who or what is walking out!

Schools are a different culture from businesses, of course, but the concept is the same. Schools have to know who is coming into the school to know what they may be walking out with or what dangers have just entered. And that is not limited to a troubled teenager with an automatic handgun and a pipe bomb.

In this section, I'm going to discuss three elements of access control that are vital. Each one may seem like a bit much, but if you analyze them, you'll see that they make sense.

Entry and Exit

The first line of defense for the school is the doors. Which doors are locked and when and who is responsible for locking them must be decided. Is it ever appropriate to prop them open, and what about the maintenance and kitchen entrances?

My opinion is that all students should be funneled through one door to start the school day. This allows for all exterior entrances to remain locked and prevent someone from sneaking in unobserved. Yes, I know that this may create a bottleneck, but let me explain a few things.

By funneling all kids through the front door with a door monitor, you'll know who is entering the school for the day. This is even more important if you are using a metal detector or hand-wanding the kids as they enter.

There should always be someone at the door to greet the kids as they enter, whether it is a security or resource officer or a member of the faculty. Will either of these know if a certain student has been expelled and not allowed to enter? Probably not, especially if there are hundreds or thousands of students, as in many of our high schools. But it is possible that a person at the door will keep unauthorized students from entering. The door greeter may know a student has been expelled or suspended.

While funneling everyone through one door, all other doors should remain locked at all times. Every school has the ability to secure the exit doors with crash bars that allow for exit in an emergency but do not allow for someone to enter without being noticed. They come in all sizes and are usually no more expensive than other types of doors.

This should apply to all doors on campus. Kitchen, delivery, and maintenance doors also have to remain locked and secured from the outside at all times. Even overhead doors need to remain in their closed, down position and locked. You're asking, "What about airflow?

It gets awful hot in the kitchen and maintenance areas." Not to worry. There is a solution.

Many areas don't have air conditioning due to the tremendous cost of installing, running, and maintaining the units or because it's only needed for a month or two of the school year. Therefore, doors are opened to allow for airflow and cooling, especially in the kitchen and maintenance sheds, where the temperature can easily top 110 degrees without airflow.

The solution is simple and relatively cheap. There are doors available that are made of wire mesh for the kitchen and some sort of chain mesh for overheads. It's the same type of heavy mesh used on catwalks and fencing. With a crash bar attached and securely installed, these doors will let air in and keep people out.

Overhead chain doors are seen in manufacturing facilities. They either come down like a regular overhead or can be attached with little effort. I have seen them utilized in manufacturing plants where the temperatures routinely get over 110 degrees during the summer. They are used specifically to increase airflow and allow some of the heat to escape at night.

I want to mention one last thing about entry and exit doors. The policy should be that they are *never* allowed to be propped open while unattended! The temptation is there to do it just once. But eventually, after a series of "just once" occasions, it becomes an unwritten policy to leave it propped open. This action defeats the entire purpose of leaving them locked; it allows for someone to enter unobserved.

If it is propped open for any reason, then someone should remain by the door at all times. This includes a monitor at recess and during deliveries. Yes, I realize what a pain in the neck this is going to be, but having someone to monitor the door—never more than twenty or thirty feet away and undistracted—is vital. This applies to the kitchen and maintenance doors as well.

Just as in your home, if you open the door to strangers, they can walk right in. You don't leave your doors unlocked and open at night while you sleep, do you? Why not? Because it makes it much easier for someone to walk in, rob you and possibly murder you and your family.

Visitors

Everyone who enters your child's school should be known to the administrative office. In order to accomplish this, you not only need a way to ensure that they come to the office—access control—but you need a way to identify them accurately once they are in and track them while in the building.

Everyone who enters the school should be required to notify the office that they are on the property and for what purpose; therefore, a system of signing in and out needs to be instituted. The policy, forms, and procedures are fairly easy to implement, but getting the staff to follow the procedures is another matter.

As with most security measures, it is tempting to ignore the rules and do the easy thing. In this case, it would be easy to bypass the visitor controls and let anyone into the building to see whomever.

A perfect analogy for this is the lock-out tag, which is used by virtually every maintenance professional I know. The lock-out tag is used whenever a piece of machinery is being worked on. It allows the maintenance person to safely work on it without the possibility of the machine being accidentally activated, injuring or killing the worker. Many times, the tags actually look like padlocks to prevent the power or start switch from being turned on.

Visitor controls are much like that lock-out tag. In order to prevent a criminal event, the policies must be adhered to. And those policies should require everyone entering school property to report to the office to sign in and to sign out. This allows the school to know who is and isn't on the property if an incident occurs.

And yes, I mean *everyone*, including delivery people making the daily delivery to the kitchen and vendors delivering a simple extension cord to the janitor. They should all be required to sign in and out, no matter how long they are there.

In the case of kitchen and maintenance deliveries, the driver should be required to sign in at the office before being allowed to enter. He should not be allowed to circumvent the system by walking through the school to get to the office, and no one else should be allowed to sign him in and out. The only exception to this is if a small delivery is made and the janitor or maintenance person meets the driver at the front door—not the back door or the maintenance door. In addition, delivery drivers should always be instructed to show their IDs when they sign in so the staff can ascertain their real identities. Yes, I know it sounds a bit paranoid and CIA-ish, but it is necessary.

Each visitor needs to sign in with his or her name, company, reason for being there, time in and out, and signature. It doesn't matter if this person is the school superintendent; everyone should sign in and get a visitor badge.

Am I out of my mind for suggesting a visitor badge? No, I'm not, and it's not as far-fetched as it may sound. It's even advisable to require an escort. By having a visitor badge, you ensure that everyone not normally at the school is identifiable to all as a visitor. Anyone who doesn't have a badge and is unfamiliar should be confronted, but more on that in a few minutes.

If visitors are escorted by whomever they came to see, you can be assured of two things: first, they are authorized to be there, and second, they will not have access to areas they shouldn't. The people escorting the visitors need to stay with them for their entire visit.

Schools must also ensure that when visitors leave the school, they sign out at the accurate time and return their visitor badges. By not signing out at the accurate time, they may be trying to place an alibi for something. I know these sounds a bit like over-the-top paranoia, but

I have seen it in the workplace and in schools. By requiring visitors to return the badge, you prevent them from reusing it the next day or some time in the future. If the school can afford them, self-expiring badges work best. But in these times of budget cuts, badges made on the computer and laminated work just fine. If a person fails to return the badge, charge $5.00 for its replacement and ensure that it is removed from the system.

Here is one last reason you should institute or encourage a visitor system in the local school. In the event of a disaster, how will anyone know who was in the school and where they were? How many people should rescue crews be looking for?

If something untoward was to occur at school, then at least the office would have the information to know if everyone has made it out or if someone is trapped. And I'm not talking about a shooting event. In the midwest and southeast regions of the country, tornados are frequent. If a school were to collapse, would you know how many to look for in a search and rescue attempt?

The same goes for other parts of the country and their potential disasters—earthquakes in California, nor'easters in New York, flash flooding anywhere, or maybe an explosion and fire. Not all explosions are caused by bombs; many are caused by gas leaks.

So while having strict control of visitors can be a major pain for everyone involved, it can save lives as well as potentially keep a major event from occurring.

Confrontation

Confrontation, unfortunately, is just as vitally necessary as the other entry control methods I talked about above.

When I talk about confrontation here, I am talking about approaching an individual who is on school property and probably shouldn't be, such as someone walking around the halls without a badge and unescorted.

These people need to be approached cautiously. First of all, you don't know if their purpose is innocuous or criminal. They may be armed with a deadly weapon, and if you confront them in an adversarial way, you may end up being the news.

The same goes for someone wandering the halls inside the school. The individual may be lost or unaware of the procedure for visitors—although it was prominently posted—or there may be a nefarious purpose to their wandering. So the importance of confronting someone in a non confrontational way is paramount.

You need to approach individuals with a hefty amount of skepticism and caution. Again, you don't know what their purpose is. Approaching them in a manner that is surly and authoritative may be what sets them off to do violence, either on campus or off. They may think you're just a total south end of a northbound donkey!

Walk up to them like you would to ask someone for directions in a shopping mall. Kindly ask them if they need something or are lost. Politely inform them that they on school property, and invite them to leave or report to the office. If they are in the halls, politely inform them of the policy and ask them to go to the office.

What happens from there will frame your next response. If they decide to get confrontational, then you can do one of three things. You can call for back-up on a two-way radio or cell phone, you can order them to leave, or you can slink off to a hole because you weren't too sure about this confrontation stuff anyway.

Any inclination toward violence or even the threat of it should be reported immediately. Using the radio or a cell phone, contact the office and request that the security or resource officer respond or that the police be called immediately.

If the individual seems disoriented, lost in a daze, confused, or otherwise impaired, you should also call the office. If this is the case, stay close until either the security or resource officer or the police arrive. This person may be experiencing a medical problem.

Whatever the issue, all persons not wearing a visitor badge and not being escorted should be confronted in the manner I described above to ensure that they follow approved policy or leave the property.

Background Screening

It should be abundantly clear that all people working around our kids should have a background check. But, unfortunately, that is not the case. While background checks will not necessarily stop a student from killing others, they will let us know who is in the school and who could possibly become violent or sexually assault our kids.

Do you realize how easy it is to work at a school and never undergo a background check? How many times have we heard about an assistant teacher or aide who assaulted a child and had never been even fingerprinted because he or she was never meant to work around kids?

Everyone who has access to the school must be checked. This means all contractors working on the new basketball arena as well as all delivery people. The school should make it mandatory for everyone coming onto school property, where kids are present or likely to be, to ensure they know who is around our kids. It can easily be worked into any contract or discussed with delivery companies.

If something untoward is found in a person's history, does that mean that the school can't hire him? Absolutely not. The school should be free to hire the best candidates. However, if the school knows a candidate's background and something does occur, at least it has a place to start looking. Of course, personnel files should remain confidential for nearly all cases.

Noncustodial Parental Sign-Out

Actually, this procedure should be used any time a student leaves school early. With the rising divorce rate and the increasing acrimony that surrounds divorces, a noncustodial parent who comes into the school and tries to remove a student should be required to do several things.

First, of course, they should sign their names and the names of the students in a sign-out book. You should always verify with the student (away from the presence of the parent) that he or she is supposed to go with that parent.

Second, the noncustodial parent must have authorization, which can take two forms. One form is written authorization from the custodial parent allowing the student to leave with the noncustodial parent. This cannot be a blanket authorization. It needs to be written, signed, and dated for every time the noncustodial parent is signing the child out of school.

The other way, which should be used only as a verification tool, is to call the custodial parent and ask for permission and verification, documenting in the sign-out book the date, time, and person spoken with. Additionally, the person making the verification cannot be a student working in the office nor a volunteer parent, only an adult employee of the school.

In the event of an emergency involving the custodial parent, the school needs to have preplanned contingencies worked out with the custodial parent on who the child is to go with and should involve law enforcement to verify that such an event has occurred.

School Building Plans and Campus Plans

Law enforcement and other emergency personnel need to have maps of the school. This is absolutely vital information for several reasons.

If a Columbine-style incident does occur, officers won't have to waste time trying to find the maps and information on the school's layout during the crisis. All public safety vehicles should carry the maps and layouts of all the schools in their area. This will allow them to easily find, clear, and rescue anyone in the school, no matter what has befallen the students.

Having the maps also helps to protect those public safety people. How? you ask. By alerting them to where all hazardous and flammable materials are used and stored, they can safely avoid those areas or direct victims away from them. Additionally, if there is a Columbine-style shooting, they can see the best way to "attack" the building and rescue injured students more efficiently. The same holds true for any type of natural disaster.

Evacuation/Notification

Every school in the country has an evacuation plan for a fire, tornado, or other such disaster. But how many of those schools also have a plan for a violent attack at the school? I would wager that most do not and that those that do have never tested it.

Likewise, all schools have warning or distress signals for a fire or some other problem. But to most administrators and teachers, the idea of someone shooting up the school is so far-fetched; it's not worth thinking about. So if the school does have a plan for such an event, who knows it?

A fire or tornado is an event that can be measured—it is not hard to know where to go. Humans are far less measured, especially when they have a list of gripes, raging hormones, and years of frustration working on them. A different type of evacuation plan is needed.

Notification plans are just as much in disarray as evacuation plans for fires and other events are. In many cases, those inside hear only bells, whistles, or tomes telling them to leave the building in a calm and orderly fashion and they have no idea what's happening.

Multiple routes of evacuation must be considered when devising a notification plan. Where do the teachers direct the kids if their quickest escape route is blocked? In the younger grades, it's up to the teachers to guide their charges out of danger. At the higher grades, the teachers need to instruct their students on where to go and hurry them along.

In some cases, especially with a violent incident, people may not be able to get out safely. But one idea may help save lives and get kids out of harm's way—rope ladders or chain ladders.

If they roll up and can be secured in a classroom, they should. These ladders will allow a whole class to evacuate an upper story quickly. Whether you think it's hokey or not, it is a viable alternative route for leaving the building,

As for notification plans, it can be just as simple. Divide the school into zones and make a notification over the intercom (not to give ideas, but most teenager shooters ignore the "command center" and go straight for revenge). Let's use my elementary school as a simple example

We had three main exits: north, south, and west. If a shooter started his attack in the basement on the west side, a PA announcement could go like this: "Level A (student with a handgun) 2W (floor and entrance)." This would simply mean that only the north and south exits should be used and that those in the middle would need to lock the door and climb out the windows.

Whether any of these will work in your child's school or not, I can't tell. The only thing I can say is that you need to demand an answer about multiple evacuation plans. As I stated before, you as a parent have the right to know if everything has been done to protect your child.

Landscaping

Most of you are probably thinking, "Huh? What does landscaping have to do with school security?" But it can be a vital and integral part of securing a school against a possible attack such as Columbine. Let me explain.

If bushes, walls, and other such landscaping prevent a clear view of areas of the school, they can also camouflage students who are planning something. Likewise, if these ornaments are close to common areas where large numbers of kids congregate, it could be a death trap. Remember that in the Columbine attack, Harris and Klebold planted propane canisters in the cafeteria area hoping to kill dozens of students. Fortunately, they failed, but maybe next time …

Bushes should be kept a minimum of three feet away from the building, allowing for at least a cursory inspection to ensure that nothing is behind them ready to surprise or harm. This also helps to prevent break-ins at older schools with basements because, again, it allows for quick discovery of such an attempt.

Walls are harder to control. Many schools have placed them around their campuses for a dual purpose. They are ornamental as well as functional—kids can sit on them to talk, eat lunch, or do other things that kids do sitting on a wall do. But walls are not transparent, and that means that bombs can be hidden behind them to kill or injure other students.

However walls are used, regular inspections must be conducted at irregular times of the unseen part of the wall. And even with that, it's not assured that anyone will catch something. A person can look at a package and never realize the potential danger, especially if that person is a teenager.

If your school utilizes these types of landscaping, you may ask them re-evaluate it. Landscaping can be used to beautify a school, but it can also be used as a tool for someone wanting to cause harm.

Chemical/Flammable Material Storage

This may sound like an area that schools would have already taken steps to protect, but I can tell you most of them have not. Volatile materials are still maintained in unlocked and unmonitored cabinets.

The maintenance shed or building is the one place where these items should be stored. At the very least, these compounds should be secured in a cabinet that is locked at all times, and even the thought of leaving it unlocked "this one time" should be guarded against. One time usually becomes common practice.

Materials should be signed out to a teacher or qualified person by a supervisor, with the sign-out and sign-in log signed by the supervisor or other administrator. The log should be checked at the end of the day to ensure that all gas cans and other items have been returned or disposed of properly. All compounds that are considered flammable can be used as accelerants.

The same goes for the science, chemistry, or other classes that may use volatile chemicals. These cannot be stored in an unlocked cabinet in the chemistry lab. There have been many cases where chemicals have been stolen by students for mischief or prank purposes without any thoughts of injuring anyone. But if someone wanted to harm others and these chemicals were easily available, why would they order off the Internet and risk being tracked?

As with maintenance and cleaning compounds, class chemicals must be locked away and accounted for at the end of the school day. They should be kept in a heavy cabinet with at least a high-security padlock. While I would prefer a security system with a keypad and alarm, I know that that most schools cannot afford that type of sophistication.

Last, these compounds should be kept away from the school in a maintenance building or shed, which needs to be as solid as possible and at least 100 feet from the school to avoid an accident that could injure to anyone. It's not as expensive as you may think. A solid, hard-to-break-into shed can be built for as little as $5,000 and schools would be wise to ask for help from the local home fix-it store and parental volunteers.

Security Systems

Many people think that schools don't need alarms in them. But just a few short years ago, we thought we didn't need locks on our doors and even left the doors open so air could flow through the house via the screen door. How many houses even have screen doors anymore except on the patio door?

Because of the world we live in, schools need to have alarm systems and even video surveillance throughout. These can stop someone from breaking into the school to steal computers, televisions, DVRs, and other equipment to pawn, not to mention other items such as those volatile chemicals.

The systems don't have to be expensive national systems. In many districts, the system can be monitored by the local police or sheriff's department. In an extreme case, the district may have to hire a security officer to monitor all of the schools in a district, who in turn dispatches the police to a particular school.

In fact, the school's maintenance department employees may be able to install the system themselves and save money that way. In addition, most of the components for systems can be purchased at electronics stores. Whether that is feasible depends on the size of the school and district, but it is an alternative for cash-strapped schools. Again, think about using donations and volunteers.

As for video surveillance systems, they are just as vital as alarms because they provide visual evidence of any wrongdoing, whether it is a break-in, an assault, or just a case of liability in a slip and fall.

Despite what most trial and corporate lawyers say, it is legal to have surveillance in any area of the school except the restrooms and locker or shower rooms. Even in those areas, they may be allowed if used appropriately.

A closed-captioned video surveillance (CCVS) system should be considered at all entry points, as well as other vital areas. Areas such as hallways, storage rooms, those with high-priced items, and even external gathering areas should be under surveillance at all times.

Let me offer one thought about video systems: they do absolutely no good unless they are monitored and recorded. Why spend thousands of dollars buying and installing a system and then not record or monitor it? A CCVS system is only as good as the other procedures in place for monitoring.

The system must be monitored twenty-four hours a day, 365 days a year. It should also be recorded with a DVR, which will allow up to 168 hours of recording per disc with images recorded every few seconds. Discs should be kept for a minimum of a year before recording over them. A security person should monitor the system during the day and during after-hours activities.

Last, alarm and video systems should be linked so that when an alarm is activated, a video record can be made of the incident. With this approach, most break-ins or other incidents can be recorded and the perpetrators caught.

A question that I am often asked is about dummy cameras. The answer is short—don't use them. If an incident occurs and a camera is present, whether dummy or real, there is an expectation of security and that someone monitoring the incident will get help on the way. With a dummy, you open yourself up to a liability suit based on that expectation.

Training

Training is one of the most cost-effective and efficient methods of instruction in the world. Training everyone involved with the school can actually save a life, and yes, I mean teaching parents the same ideas as teachers when it comes to dealing with school violence.

I am a firm advocate of the Socratic Method of teaching. This involves asking the students to participate and, in some cases, literally teach themselves by voicing their answers and thinking out loud. In my training business, I have found it to be most useful.

According to the Society for Human Resource Management (SHRM), in a study conducted years ago, instructor-based classes allow for greater retention of the information being presented. And when the learners actively participate, the retention is even higher.

Understanding how harried educational staff is today, I recommend that sessions last no more than two hours. Preferably, each training subject should be covered in 15–30 minutes, but some subjects will require more time, such as the warning signs of school violence. In lieu of such short time periods, frequent breaks should be proffered.

I am very much against teaching methods that involve nothing but watching videos, listening to CDs, or reading manuals. For the most part, unless an instructor is in tune with the subject matter, then the longer the video or CD goes on, the less the participants are actually paying attention and retaining. And if that is the case, the class may satisfy the liability requirements, but the teachers will be no better informed and the school will have wasted money on it.

For teachers, I always recommend that they be tested after the class is over. Why? Because it doesn't do much good to take the time and money to train people and then not ensure that they learned from it.

Arizona state law says that all those wishing to be security guards attend an eight hour class on how to do the job right, but they require no testing. So meeting the requirement gets the guard company off the hook for any screw-ups, but it does little for the contracting company or the guard. I always test those in my independent guard classes.

When training parents, a straight, thorough session that lasts no more than two hours is best. This allows them to get in and get out quickly so they can resume their busy lives. Unfortunately, you'll never know how much they have retained until an incident occurs.

Various governmental agencies offer training in this area, but I find them lacking in solutions to the problem. Furthermore, almost none of the Web sites I've looked at in preparing this book address the problem of violence in the schools from a preventive standpoint.

While there are classes on bullying, drug and alcohol abuse, and gangs, these are not the only causes of violence. Not a single class I found was dedicated to learning the warning signs, which to me is appalling.

So schools are left with wringing their hands and doing nothing. Even those with plans in place have best practices sections that run dozens of pages, and they're written in "governmentese," which is nearly impossible to interpret. In all honesty, they should be less than a quarter of their size and written in plain English.

Again, training is one of the most cost-effective ways to accomplish something in the effort to prevent violence. However, it doesn't do anyone any good to spend hundreds of thousands of dollars on programs that are flawed from the beginning. Why would you want to add new hinges and locks to the barn door after the horses have left and the walls have collapsed?

When it comes to preventing violence in our schools and safeguarding the lives of our children, we can say an ounce of prevention is truly worth a pound of cure.

Forming a Crisis Management Team

Most of you who work for a school district are going to say that your district already has a crisis management team (CMT) in place, and most of you who are parents are asking, "What?"

Parents who are not involved in management will have little idea of what a true CMT can or will do for them after an incident. They may have heard of some sort of plan at their workplaces, but seldom does the owner-ship or management let them in on the secret, sometimes fearing it'll be overused.

Teachers and administrators within a school or school district usually have and are aware of a plan of action involving a CMT after an incident. But what I am addressing is the actual formation and optimization of such a team.

When forming a CMT, the most important thing to determine is who is involved with the creation of the committee and who will have input on the project. And as you can probably tell from the rest of the book, I have some unconventional ideas about that.

To create the best-laid plan in response to a deadly incident at a school, a wide array of people should be used. I mean that everyone at your disposal should be used to create your plan and team.

Teachers and school administrators should obviously be utilized. And of course district administrators will be called in, not to mention the district's security people.

But, additionally, when forming your plan and determining who is to be on the response team to handle the aftermath, students and parents should be involved as well. It's not quite as crazy as it sounds. Let me explain.

By having students on your creation committee, you will take into consideration their concerns regarding such an incident. Because they bring such a unique perspective of the world, they can bring the same perspective to the planning process, addressing things that adults may not even think of or about. What is important to us is not necessarily what is important to a teenager.

Many school districts couldn't care less about what parents have to say, much less their teens. But again, the parents will bring a different perspective to the planning. Schools will be planning, mainly, on getting counselors and repair crews dispatched and focusing on getting back to normal. With parental involvement, the team can witness the emotional response not after an incident but before, which is when you want it so you can plan for it.

Let's not forget to include someone from the support staff in this planning as well. Support staff? Yes, janitors, cooks, secretaries, aides, and the like need to be in on the planning. They will be in the school at the same time as everyone else, so why shouldn't they help plan? They have just as much to lose as anyone else.

After you've created the disaster recovery plan (DRP) and have the CMT in place, there is one last thing to do—test it. It does you absolutely no good to spend months of planning and money on this if you don't test it. What good is a Lamborghini if you never drive it? By testing it in a controlled manner, you'll find out what does and doesn't work and what needs to be deleted, added, or clarified. This is going to be set in place for you when the real thing happens, and that is not the time to see if your plan works.

In the past, some people have asked me if I was nuts to add teenagers and parents to this mix, and I assure you that I am not. The emotional response you'll get from both students and parents during this sort of crisis will help you understand the need to have calm and reassuring procedures in place, not chaos.

By dealing with student and parental volunteers, some of whom have "real world experience," we're tapping into skills and knowledge we might never know about or be throwing out. And as institutions of learning, are schools not supposed to instruct teenagers on gathering as much useful information as possible before finalizing a plan and understanding a process?

Transparency

As a parent, I have tried to get information from my school district on violent incidents. I have been told several times that the district doesn't keep track of that information, which means "None of your business, that information is kept somewhere else." And then, of course, there's always the popular response, "I can take a message and have that person call you back."

None of these answers is adequate. The overall concern here is the cloak of secrecy kept over the problems at a school, and I believe the answer is very simple.

Administrators and bureaucrats in the district offices do not want the extent of the problem known. In many cases, it will open them up to lawsuits. In just as many cases, the administrators will lose their bonuses if they have too many incidents. Think I'm joking?

An incident took place in Baltimore in which a teacher was physically attacked by a student in a classroom, with others watching, and it was caught on film. The teacher was beaten so severely that she had to be taken out by stretcher, with the student still screaming and attempting to hit her. After several days in the hospital, she called the police department and requested a report. She was informed that no report existed because no call was issued.

When the principal was confronted with this, he simply stated, "I didn't think it would have been appropriate." The teacher, outraged, made her own report and notified the media. After some investigation, the principal admitted that reporting the incident could have caused him to lose his bonus. How many times are attacks like these this not reported to police or the media?

In 2005, a Philadelphia school district launched an audit of the assaults reported. The number reported at one high school was just over 800 incidents a year, but the actual number was over 3,200. For what purpose were incidents so underreported? We don't know because a formal investigation was never launched.

This is one reason that I take any numbers on assaults and bullying provided by educational institutions with a grain of salt. My belief is that the State of Arizona's reported 20,000 incidents are underreported by as much as 75 percent.

The way to combat this and ensure accurate reporting of the number of assaults and bullying incidents is for administration to keep a ledger. It should be available for public inspection, and names do not have to be used.

Only the number and type of incidents should be kept. For examples, the ledger should include weapons found—handguns, knives, pepper spray, stun guns, etc.—and drugs, both prescription and over the counter. These numbers, along with records of suspensions, detentions, and expulsions, would be a great help.

And as with all other communication issues, all incidents known to teachers, counselors, and administrators should also be marked down, after checking to ensure there is no duplication. The number should reflect the actual number of incidents, not the number of students.

In the case of bullying in Arizona—20,000 incidents in one year—only the number of students involved was reported, not the number of incidents. That could cause the number to be much higher, possibly in the hundreds of thousands.

Schools and districts should also be more transparent on other issues. If a program is cut because of budgetary concerns, you have the right to know how much was doled out in pay raises. You are also entitled to being told why rule changes are being put in place.

Should the district release all information about these things? Absolutely not. Many things are confidential. For example, if a student was found with a handgun on campus and the rules were changed to address the issue, the details of what happened, the school involved, and the student's name should be released.

Speaking of this brings up whether parents be notified of all potential threats to the school or its students. The proverbial letter home should be sent any time an incident occurs that threatens the safety of our kids.

If a student is caught with a handgun, a letter should be sent home. If a threat is graffiti on a wall, as you will read later, it probably shouldn't be broadcast. If a student is found with a hit or death list, absolutely the letter should be sent, and the parents of those on the list should be called in.

Last, we come to a controversial topic.

Zero Tolerance

This phrase should be used carefully and, if possible, with a large dose of common sense, which most schools don't seem to possess with regard to this term.

If a six-year-old comes to school with a plastic butter knife to spread something, that's not a weapon—it's a butter knife! Don't suspend the poor kid just send a note home informing the parents that it is not a good idea to bring such a thing to school. On the other hand, if the knife is a serrated steak knife, then there is cause for concern.

As parents or teachers, you need to know your children, even teenagers. If one student says to another, "I'm gonna kick your butt from one end of the parking lot to the other," is it a threat or is it just two friends joking around? Unless you know your children, then you won't know and have to assume the worst. So before the zero-tolerance phrase is tossed around, find out about the children first.

These measures are just the starting point. Ask your school if they do these things and if they don't, then ask why and press until you get an answer. As parents, you have a right to know what measures are being used to safeguard your children.

Chapter 6

What Not to Do

There are several things that should never be done when confronted by a shooter in your hallways. And of course, we never want to put our crisis management team into use, nor do we want to put our dusty evacuation plan into action either.

But there will come a day when it will be necessary. We all hope that it is only a bluff, but too frequently we hear of a school somewhere that has been evacuated for some violent incident, such as a bomb threat or fire, or that has gone into lockdown mode because someone doesn't want to get a real job and decides to rob and steal from others.

There are many thoughts and ideas floating around out there about what our teenagers and teachers should do during an attack. Some say fight back, while others instruct them to stay put and hide as best they can. Still others want to allow handguns onto campuses under a concealed carry law.

Well, who'd have thought it—I have some strong ideas and thoughts on this subject as well!

Fighting Back

The last thing that I would want our children to do if an incident occurs is to fight.

This will, I am fully convinced, get them killed. Of course, every parent would be proud if their kid stood up and became the hero, like the passengers on Flight 93, but that isn't likely to happen.

We are discussing teenagers who usually will freak out when they get into a car accident with their parents' cars. I don't believe that 13- to 18-year-olds are capable of making the split-second decisions necessary to effectively fight back. I am not saying our teens aren't intelligent; they've just not been trained.

So should we train them? How could we get teens to learn how to take on a 9mm or AK47 when we can barely get them to focus and concentrate on the Civil War? Some teens are capable of doing this—they're called *soldiers.*

In 2006, Butler County, Texas, received a grant from the federal government—our tax dollars at work—to study the effectiveness of teaching students how to fight back against an armed intruder and determine whether this was a good idea or not and which form of fighting back would be most effective. Unfortunately, there are other security experts who back and endorse this method.

Many of our teenagers do rash and stupid things when pressured. Many of them can do only three things after a car accident, even if no one is seriously hurt.

- They begin crying and can't speak. This generally happens with girls, but not exclusively.
- They sit quietly and acquiesce to everything they are being told in silent submission. You've seen them at accident sites—the teenage boy with shoulders slumped and head hung low while talking to the police officer.
- They think only one thing: "Oh my God, my parents are going to kill me!" Whether it's the family car or not, parents always thank God that the kids are alive and unhurt, but then the nurturing instinct comes out and they say, "What were you thinking? How fast were you going? Who was in the car? Were you smoking again?" And as parents we know we'll use interrogation techniques banned by the United Nations Human Rights Commission because, after all, they're our kids and we love them.

In a shooting incident, throwing books, chairs, desks, or other such items is nonsense. All that will do is make assailants even angrier. They will already be angry at the world and suicidal, so encouraging them will not help.

If these kids become angrier, then there is a distinct possibility that they will continue their shooting for a longer period. I don't mean to seem cold-hearted and callous, but if these shooters kill themselves sooner rather than later, we all benefit by having fewer dead teenagers on the evening news. And even with empathy and sorrow for the shooter's parents, isn't that why you're reading this book?

My point is simple: books, staplers, and desks may have an outside chance of bringing a shooter back into reality or disabling them. But why should we endanger our kids even more by teaching them to try something with such a low probability of success? We'd never try it in our private lives or in business, so why should we try with our greatest loves?

Firearms on Campus

Even more ridiculous to me than teaching our kids to fight someone with an automatic weapon is allowing anyone with a concealed carry weapon (CCW) permit to carry a weapon on school property. There are many arguments against this, so let me get onto my soapbox and get started.

Do not get me wrong. I am all for the proliferation of handguns in properly licensed hands, and I am a strong believer in the Second Amendment. While I'm not a member of the National Rifle Association, I believe in everyone's right to own and carry firearms. After all, I live in Arizona, where we can openly carry firearms on our hips and walk down the street.

But I draw the line at allowing handguns in our schools, even if the individual is licensed to legally carry a gun in a purse or briefcase. But as with many things in real life, there is an exception to every rule and I think it's a good one.

If someone is afraid for his or her life due to a specific threat, then let them carry. A prime example of this is a woman who has a restraining order against a former boyfriend or husband. If she can show a true threat to her person, then she should be allowed to carry. The same goes for a man as well.

My objection to a blanket decision to allow CCW's on campus has several facets, as you can tell. But the first is that the certification training for a CCW is not very stringent, just four hours of classroom and four hours on the range. It doesn't matter if they can hit the center of target; just getting it onto the target is good enough. (I'm reminded of a quote I use in my customer service training 'The best isn't and Good enough never is').

In addition, people who get CCW permits are not required to reapply or requalify for several years. Police officers, on the other hand, have to qualify every few months as a rule. I know the argument: police officers are more likely to use their sidearms than a citizen. That's true, but the police also enter areas that we never would, even with a firearm. There are states that have more stringent requirements for their CCW permits, but I stand firm.

School employees are subject to background checks, but those don't reveal anything about their behavior. We've seen numerous teachers or other school staff members being arraigned for murder, rape, or child molestation. These people all passed through the screening process, didn't they?

If there is a shooting on school property and everyone is allowed to carry a weapon, let us ponder these scenarios, if you will.

Preciously sweet sixty-year-old Mrs. Thompson is a teacher. She's five-foot nothing and weighs ninety-eight pounds. She carries a handgun because it's allowed and she feels threatened by some of her students during class. A conversation is overheard or a glint of metal is seen in her purse by a student.

Now consider that Mrs. Thompson is accosted by several hormonally charged male students in the parking lot. Now a beloved teacher is hospitalized or dead and a handgun is on the loose, possibly on campus. And it's not just teachers like Mrs. Thompson who are in danger. Not many football players or physical education instructors can beat off several teenagers at once, especially if the attackers are bound and determined to take a firearm.

Now let's consider the example of Mr. Jenkins, a young and virile new teacher. He's twenty-four years old but looks seventeen and is so good-looking that the song "Don't Stand So Close to Me" could have been written with him in mind. He has a CCW permit and has his weapon with him at school.

An incident occurs, and he becomes the hero of the day when he shoots and kills the rampaging student, who was able to cause only a minor injury to another student. The police arrive and see the seventeen-year-old-looking Mr. Jenkins standing close to the body of the shooter. They command him to stop and turn around. He automatically obeys, with the pistol still in his hand. The officer feels threatened and fires three shots into his center body mass, and now the hero of the day is also one of the dead.

Bookish science teacher Mr. Hollister is carrying a weapon because he can. When conducting his class, he hears gunfire in the hallway. He tells his students to hold on while he investigates. In the hallway, he sees several students running in a panic. He observes another student with what appears to be a handgun. Mr. Hollister takes out his gun and fires three shots—he practices all the time. The student is killed, and Mr. Hollister is the hero until it's learned that the "handgun" was a micro cassette recorder and the shots heard were actually doors slamming down the hall.

Now a student is dead and Mr. Hollister, who practiced so hard, is arrested for murder, no longer the hero but the goat.

Let us try this scenario. The above -mentioned Mr. Jenkins steps out of his class and shoots the student who was killing targeting the other students. Then Mr. Hollister steps out of his classroom to see a young man standing over another student who looks dead, and he fires his gun, killing the young Mr. Jenkins in a panic.

I know what you're thinking: these are scenarios that would never happen. Maybe I'm using scare tactics to push my point. Well, yes, I am using these nightmarish scenarios to push my point, but these are very possible. They could happen.

Maybe by demonstrating these nightmares, a student or other innocent person will be prevented from being killed in the hallways of our schools. I would rather try to scare you into thinking my way than hear about another child being killed in school by another child, a teacher, or anyone else.

I am not totally against a few people being able to carry their personal handguns into our schools. But I do believe that there should be some tighter restrictions in place over who can carry, when they can carry, and why they can carry a concealed weapon.

Teachers, administrators, and support staff haven't been trained in crisis management, or as I call it, in combat mode. They have been taught how to instruct young minds in the areas of history, mathematics, writing, and the like. They have never been instructed on how to handle a crisis or combat situation.

It is that lack of training that makes *most* staff likely to become part of the tragedy rather than part of preventing one. These people are very intelligent, and they generally know their subjects well and can teach them well. But asking someone who has never been trained in crisis or combat response to think in a clear, logical way during a shooting is pointless. The only people who should be allowed to carry a firearm into the halls of learning are those who have either the experience or the training to handle crisis situations.

School resource officers and ex-military or police officers are the ones that come to mind. And teachers, administrators, or other support personnel who are willing to submit themselves to that type of training are also acceptable.

But even with this training, there is no guarantee that a tragedy will be averted. Many are the cases in which a resource officer or other armed individual was unable to prevent a shooting or was disabled. These people make mistakes just like anyone else, but they face the public expectation to be perfect.

CHH

We talked about the Can't Happen Here (CHH) attitude earlier under things that foster violence. It is one of the attitudes that we can't allow ourselves to fall into. Of all the things we shouldn't do, this may be the biggest one.

Saying that something can't happen here is tantamount to inviting it to happen! For example, I have a friend who is extremely overweight (he says fat). If someone tells him that food is on the counter or anywhere else for that matter, he takes it as a challenge. The all-you-can-eat buffets shutter the doors when he approaches because he considers them a challenge. How much can a fat man eat?

Random chance is an aspect of this attitude. Look at Murphy's Law—if something can happen, it will happen and at the worst possible moment. We should prepare for that, especially the possibility of losing our future to a shooter who is high on adrenaline, anger, and hormones.

School violence reaches virtually every school and district. Maybe no one is spraying the halls with an M-16 in a certain district, but it does have bullying, teasing, fistfights, and other such violence going on. This includes pranks such as smoke bombs, firecrackers, and pulling the fire alarm. No school is immune.

And the more we think that it can't happen here, the more likely it is that something catastrophic will happen at our children's schools or within the district. As parents, teachers, and administrators, we need to wake up and smell the gun powder.

What to Do

If a student does get a weapon into school and begins to threaten others with it, I say do the cowardly thing—*run*.

Students should not attempt to fight back or look behind them. They need to be evacuated from the building as soon as the alarm goes off or even the suspicion is raised.

If the students cannot evacuate the building the normal way, then they need to barricade the doors to the classroom as thoroughly as possible in an effort to delay the perpetrator. By delaying the shooter, they will force him to move on to another target, and hopefully there won't be any.

Additionally, for those classrooms that are several stories high and possibly too risky to evacuate, rope ladders should be employed to allow the students to leave the building.

After evacuating, the students need to move as far as possible away from the building. This is to prevent the shooter from having multiple targets within easy weapon range, whatever that may be. Additionally, teachers should have accurate and timely rosters of who was actually present in their classes.

You must instruct your children that if they do get caught in a classroom with a shooter, they must follow the instructions of the gunman at all times. It doesn't matter if they want to do what the shooter wants or not; they are less likely to get shot if they comply and not irritate someone who is already agitated and strung as tight as a high wire. Have them do exactly as the shooter says because, at that point, they have only a fifty-fifty chance of survival.

Being a security professional and one who never wants to sugarcoat a potentially bad situation, I've probably scared the holy living hell out of you by now. If I've done that, then I've done what I set out to do.

I hope that I've given you something to ponder and something to discuss with your spouse, children, and your children's schools. I want all children to grow up.

Again, unfortunately, we cannot ensure that nothing will ever happen. Prison walls, guard towers, metal detectors, and searches at our schools are not what any of us want. And yet, even though we still couldn't guarantee their safety with those protections in place, the knee-jerk reaction is to install them anyway.

As parents, we need to know our children well enough to know when something's wrong. We need to be involved with the whos, whats, wheres, whens, whys, and hows of their dates, their schools, their rooms, and their computers. Yes, I know that cuts against the grain, but it must be done or it could be you on the evening news saying, "He was a good kid. We didn't know what he was planning."

School educators and administrators need to encourage kids to be kids. But they also need to intervene when bullying goes too far or if there is a threat against a student or teacher. Don't sweep it under the rug. Things like this smell bad enough as it is, but it gets much worse if the rug has to be pulled back to clean up the blood.

Conclusion

We're at the end of this book. And I hope that together we help to prevent violence in our schools. It is a problem we need to address before more of our teenagers fall victim to another Columbine.

I've talked about a lot of different things and a lot of different ways to help in prevention. Some of you will think of these as harsh and reeking of fascism. In some respects, you may be right.

I can only present my views and the results of my research, investigation, and experience. I can't make you think like me, nor can I make you believe in the way I do things.

What I do know is that there are things we can do to stop our kids from being victims of violence in the one place outside of home where they should be safe. If you find a better way than what I've set forth here, then more power to you.

But, if nothing else, what I want you take away from this book are the fundamentals:

- Parents are responsible for their children while they live at home and for everything they do.
- Parents needs to instill a sense of responsibility in their children
- Schools and administrators need to be more transparent in their dealings with the public and with taxpayers.
- Schools need to take more responsibility for what goes on inside their walls.
- More training in security practices needs to be done.
- The warning signs of potential teens are of paramount importance

Last, and here comes that word again, *communication* is the most important tool in preventing bullying and violence in our schools. No, it's not easy to establish. And yes, it takes continual effort, but the rewards of knowing your children and other students are very much worth the effort.

Going back to the beginning, not every teenager who is faced with a multitude of problems will assault anyone else. I was bullied and teased incessantly from seventh grade to eleventh and yet I didn't assault, kill, or do harm to anyone else. And I turned out okay (well, maybe not okay—I've been told I am a little off-center sometimes, but we'll save that discussion for another day).

We as parents want to keep our children as safe as possible. I'm sure that we'd like to put them in bubble wrap to keep them safe from playground bumps and bruises, and we'd like to put them in a cocoon so that none of the emotional pressures hurt them either. But we can't.

We can surround our schools with walls, guard towers, barbed wire, and armed guards, but we still couldn't keep our kids safe from violence. In fact, unless we chain them to desks and drug them silly, they will all find a way to hurt one another through teasing and bullying.

What we can do is take appropriate steps and measures to limit what occurs or starts at school. By doing that, both at home and at school, we can keep our children safer so they can grow up, make lots of money saving the world, and take care of us in our old age.

Appendix

Time Line of Worldwide School Shootings

Feb. 2, 1996 Moses Lake, Wash.	Two students and one teacher killed, one other wounded when 14-year-old Barry Loukaitis opened fire on his algebra class.
March 13, 1996 Dunblane, Scotland	16 children and one teacher killed at Dunblane Primary School by Thomas Hamilton, who then killed himself. 10 others wounded in attack.
Feb. 19, 1997 Bethel, Alaska	Principal and one student killed, two others wounded by Evan Ramsey, 16.
March 1997 Sanaa, Yemen	Eight people (six students and two others) at two schools killed by Mohammad Ahman al-Naziri.
Oct. 1, 1997 Pearl, Miss.	Two students killed and seven wounded by Luke Woodham, 16, who was also accused of killing his mother. He and his friends were said to be outcasts who worshiped Satan.
Dec. 1, 1997 West Paducah, Ky.	Three students killed, five wounded by Michael Carneal, 14, as they participated in a prayer circle at Heath High School.
Dec. 15, 1997 Stamps, Ark.	Two students wounded. Colt Todd, 14, was hiding in the woods when he shot the students as they stood in the parking lot.

March 24, 1998 Jonesboro, Ark.	Four students and one teacher killed, ten others wounded outside as Westside Middle School emptied during a false fire alarm. Mitchell Johnson, 13, and Andrew Golden, 11, shot at their classmates and teachers from the woods.
April 24, 1998 Edinboro, Pa.	One teacher, John Gillette, killed, two students wounded at a dance at James W. Parker Middle School. Andrew Wurst, 14, was charged.
May 19, 1998 Fayetteville, Tenn.	One student killed in the parking lot at Lincoln County High School three days before he was to graduate. The victim was dating the ex-girlfriend of his killer, 18-year-old honor student Jacob Davis.
May 21, 1998 Springfield, Ore.	Two students killed, 22 others wounded in the cafeteria at Thurston High School by 15-year-old Kip Kinkel. Kinkel had been arrested and released a day earlier for bringing a gun to school. His parents were later found dead at home.
June 15, 1998 Richmond, Va.	One teacher and one guidance counselor wounded by a 14-year-old boy in the school hallway.
April 20, 1999 Littleton, Colo.	14 students (including killers) and one teacher killed, 23 others wounded at Columbine High School in the nation's deadliest school shooting. Eric Harris, 18, and Dylan Klebold, 17, had plotted for a year to kill at least 500 and blow up their school. At the end of their hour-long rampage, they turned their guns on themselves.

April 28, 1999 Taber, Alberta, Canada	One student killed, one wounded at W. R. Myers High School in first fatal high school shooting in Canada in 20 years. The suspect, a 14-year-old boy, had dropped out of school after he was severely ostracized by his classmates.
May 20, 1999 Conyers, Ga.	Six students injured at Heritage High School by Thomas Solomon, 15, who was reportedly depressed after breaking up with his girlfriend.
Nov. 19, 1999 Deming, N.M.	Victor Cordova Jr., 12, shot and killed Araceli Tena, 13, in the lobby of Deming Middle School.
Dec. 6, 1999 Fort Gibson, Okla.	Four students wounded as Seth Trickey, 13, opened fire with a 9mm semiautomatic handgun at Fort Gibson Middle School.
Dec. 7, 1999 Veghel, Netherlands	One teacher and three students wounded by a 17-year-old student.
Feb. 29, 2000 Mount Morris Township, Mich.	Six-year-old Kayla Rolland shot dead at Buell Elementary School near Flint, Mich. The assailant was identified as a six-year-old boy with a .32-caliber handgun.
March 2000 Branneburg, Germany	One teacher killed by a 15-year-old student, who then shot himself. The shooter has been in a coma ever since.
March 10, 2000 Savannah, Ga.	Two students killed by Darrell Ingram, 19, while leaving a dance sponsored by Beach High School.

May 26, 2000 Lake Worth, Fla.	One teacher, Barry Grunow, shot and killed at Lake Worth Middle School by Nate Brazill, 13, with .25-caliber semiautomatic pistol on the last day of classes.
Sept. 26, 2000 New Orleans, La.	Two students wounded with the same gun during a fight at Woodson Middle School.
Jan. 17, 2001 Baltimore, Md.	One student shot and killed in front of Lake Clifton Eastern High School.
Jan. 18, 2001 Jan, Sweden	One student killed by two boys, ages 17 and 19.
March 5, 2001 Santee, Calif.	Two killed and 13 wounded by Charles Andrew Williams, 15, firing from a bathroom at Santana High School.
March 7, 2001 Williamsport, Pa.	Elizabeth Catherine Bush, 14, wounded student Kimberly Marchese in the cafeteria of Bishop Neumann High School; she was depressed and frequently teased.
March 22, 2001 Granite Hills, Calif.	One teacher and three students wounded by Jason Hoffman, 18, at Granite Hills High School. A policeman shot and wounded Hoffman.
March 30, 2001 Gary, Ind.	One student killed by Donald R. Burt, Jr., a 17-year-old student who had been expelled from Lew Wallace High School.
Nov. 12, 2001 Caro, Mich.	Chris Buschbacher, 17, took two hostages at the Caro Learning Center before killing himself.
Jan. 15, 2002 New York, N.Y.	A teenager wounded two students at Martin Luther King Jr. High School.

Feb. 19, 2002 Freising, Germany	Two killed in Eching by a man at the factory from which he had been fired; he then traveled to Freising and killed the headmaster of the technical school from which he had been expelled. He also wounded another teacher before killing himself.
April 26, 2002 Erfurt, Germany	13 teachers, two students, and one policeman killed, ten wounded by Robert Steinhaeuser, 19, at the Johann Gutenberg secondary school. Steinhaeuser then killed himself.
April 29, 2002 Vlasenica, Bosnia-Herzegovina	One teacher killed, one wounded by Dragoslav Petkovic, 17, who then killed himself.
October 28, 2002 Tucson, Ariz.	Robert S. Flores Jr., 41, a student at the nursing school at the University of Arizona, shot and killed three female professors and then himself.
April 14, 2003 New Orleans, La.	One 15-year-old killed, and three students wounded at John McDonogh High School by gunfire from four teenagers (none were students at the school). The motive was gang-related.
April 24, 2003 Red Lion, Pa.	James Sheets, 14, killed principal Eugene Segro of Red Lion Area Junior High School before killing himself.
Sept. 24, 2003 Cold Spring, Minn.	Two students are killed at Rocori High School by John Jason McLaughlin, 15.
Sept. 28, 2004 Carmen de Patagones, Argentina	Three students killed and 6 wounded by a 15-year-old Argentininan student in a town 620 miles south of Buenos Aires.

March 21, 2005 Red Lake, Minn.	Jeff Weise, 16, killed grandfather and companion, then arrived at school where he killed a teacher, a security guard, 5 students, and finally himself, leaving a total of 10 dead.
Nov. 8, 2005 Jacksboro, Tenn.	One 15-year-old shot and killed an assistant principal at Campbell County High School and seriously wounded two other administrators.
Aug. 24, 2006 Essex, Vt.	Christopher Williams, 27, looking for his ex-girlfriend at Essex Elementary School, shot two teachers, killing one and wounding another. Before going to the school, he had killed the ex-girlfriend's mother.
Sept. 13, 2006 Montreal, Canada	Kimveer Gill, 25, opened fire with a semiautomatic weapon at Dawson College. Anastasia De Sousa, 18, died and more than a dozen students and faculty were wounded before Gill killed himself.
Sept. 27, 2006 Bailey, Colo.	Adult male held six students hostage at Platte Canyon High School and then shot and killed Emily Keyes, 16, and himself.
Sept. 29, 2006 Cazenovia, Wis.	A 15-year-old student shot and killed Weston School principal John Klang.
Oct. 3, 2006 Nickel Mines, Pa.	32-year-old Carl Charles Roberts IV entered the one-room West Nickel Mines Amish School and shot 10 schoolgirls, ranging in age from 6 to 13 years old, and then himself. Five of the girls and Roberts died.
Jan. 3, 2007 Tacoma, Wash.	Douglas Chanthabouly, 18, shot fellow student Samnang Kok, 17, in the hallway of Henry Foss High School.

April 16, 2007 Blacksburg, Va.	A 23-year-old Virginia Tech student, Cho Seung-Hui, killed two in a dorm, then killed 30 more 2 hours later in a classroom building. His suicide brought the death toll to 33, making the shooting rampage the most deadly in U.S. history. Fifteen others were wounded.
Sept. 21, 2007 Dover, Del.	A Delaware State Univesity Freshman, Loyer D. Brandon, shot and wounded two other Freshman students on the University campus. Brandon is being charged with attempted murder, assault, reckless engagement, as well as a gun charge.
Oct. 10, 2007 Cleveland, Ohio	A 14-year-old student at a Cleveland high school, Asa H. Coon, shot and injured two students and two teachers before he shot and killed himself. The victims' injuries were not life-threatening.
Nov. 7, 2007 Tuusula, Finland	An 18-year-old student in southern Finland shot and killed five boys, two girls, and the female principal at Jokela High School. At least 10 others were injured. The gunman shot himself and died from his wounds in the hospital.
Feb. 8, 2008 Baton Rouge, Louisiana	A nursing student shot and killed two women and then herself in a classroom at Louisiana Technical College in Baton Rouge.
Feb. 11, 2008 Memphis, Tennessee	A 17-year-old student at Mitchell High School shot and wounded a classmate in gym class.

Feb. 12, 2008 Oxnard, California	A 14-year-old boy shot a student at E.O. Green Junior High School causing the 15-year-old victim to be brain dead.
Feb. 14, 2008 DeKalb, Illinois	Gunman kills five students and then himself, and wounds 17 more when he opens fire on a classroom at Northern Illinois University. The gunman, Stephen P. Kazmierczak, was identified as a former graduate student at the university in 2007.
Sept. 23, 2008 Kauhajoki, Finland	A 20-year-old male student shot and killed at least nine students and himself at a vocational college in Kauhajok, 330km (205 miles) north of the capital, Helsinki.
Nov. 12, 2008 Fort Lauderdale, Florida	A 15-year-old female student was shot and killed by a classmate at Dillard High School in Fort Lauderdale
Source: "A Time Line of Recent Worldwide School Shootings," InfoPlease.com. <http://www.infoplease.com/ipa/A0777958.html>